**How to Pass**

# NATIONAL 5
# Lifeskills
# Maths

Mike Smith

**HODDER**
**GIBSON**
AN HACHETTE UK COMPANY

The Publishers would like to thank the following for permission to reproduce copyright material:

**Photo credits** Igor Mojzes/Fotolia, p. vi; Beatrice Preve/Fotolia, p. 9; M. Schuppich/Fotolia, p. 13; Dragonimages/Fotolia, p. 14; Sima/Fotolia, p. 24; Finnegan/Fotolia, p. 27; Flafabri/Fotolia, p. 30; Dudarev Mikhail/Fotolia, p. 36; Whitelook/Fotolia, p. 39; WavebreakMediaMicro, p. 42; Topae/Fotolia, p. 53; OZMedia/Fotolia, p. 53; Ikonoklast_hh/Fotolia, p. 81

**Acknowledgements** The tables on pp. 93–97 and those on pp. 98–100 are reproduced by kind permission of the Scottish Qualifications Authority.

Although every effort has been made to ensure that website addresses are correct at time of going to press, Hodder Gibson cannot be held responsible for the content of any website mentioned in this book. It is sometimes possible to find a relocated web page by typing in the address of the home page for a website in the URL window of your browser.

Hachette UK's policy is to use papers that are natural, renewable and recyclable products and made from wood grown in sustainable forests. The logging and manufacturing processes are expected to conform to the environmental regulations of the country of origin.

Orders: please contact Bookpoint Ltd, 130 Park Drive, Abingdon, Oxon OX14 4SE. Telephone: (44) 01235 827720. Fax: (44) 01235 400454. Lines are open 9.00–5.00, Monday to Saturday, with a 24-hour message answering service. Visit our website at www.hoddereducation.co.uk. Hodder Gibson can be contacted direct on: Tel: 0141 848 1609; Fax: 0141 889 6315; email: hoddergibson@hodder.co.uk

© Mike Smith 2014

First published in 2014 by
Hodder Gibson, an imprint of Hodder Education
An Hachette UK Company
2a Christie Street
Paisley PA1 1NB

| Impression number | 5 | 4 | 3 | 2 | 1 |
|---|---|---|---|---|---|
| Year | 2018 | 2017 | 2016 | 2015 | 2014 |

Cover photo © viperagp/Fotolia
Illustrations by Aptara, Inc.
Typeset in Cronos Pro 13/15 by Aptara, Inc.
Printed in Spain
A catalogue record for this title is available from the British Library
ISBN: 978 1 4718 0148 8

# Contents

# Welcome to *How To Pass National 5 Lifeskills Maths*

By the time you are reading this, you are probably well on the way to completing the National 5 Lifeskills Mathematics course. Over the period of time you have been following this course, you will have been building on your previous mathematical knowledge and learning some new skills.

Now, perhaps, it is time to practise some exam skills and techniques. The good news is that, as in many areas of life, the more you practise the better you get!

In this book you will find:
- key words and vocabulary
- worked examples with explanations and tips
- exam techniques, hints and tips
- 'what to look out for'
- 'what you should know'

You may have chosen this course for a variety of reasons:
- You have successfully completed National 4 Lifeskills Mathematics, or National 4 Mathematics.
- You wish to add to your 'portfolio' of National 5 qualifications.
- You think that this course is relevant to your other subjects and your future education or career.

You may have noticed that the skills you are learning in this course are transferable. That is, they are all useful tools, both in other subjects and in all walks of life — skills that you will use over and over again. These include:
- reasoning
- interpretation of a problem
- analysis of a problem
- justification of a solution
- communication

# The course outline

National 5 Lifeskills Mathematics consists of three units:
- Managing finance and statistics (FS)
- Geometry and measures (GM)
- Numeracy and data handling (ND)

To achieve a course award you must pass all three units and the exam. The units are pass/fail and the exam is graded A–D. To achieve an A you must show a consistently high standard of answer.

The content of each unit is set out below.

| Managing finance and statistics | Geometry and measures | Numeracy and data |
|---|---|---|
| Finance:<br>● Budgeting<br>● Balancing income and outgoings<br>● Income and deductions<br>● Determining best deal<br>● Currency exchange<br>● Interest rates<br>● Savings and borrowings | Geometry:<br>● Gradient<br>● Area of composite shapes<br>● Volume of composite solids<br>● Pythagoras (two-stage) | Numeracy:<br>● Notation<br>● Significant figures/ decimal places<br>● Fractions/decimals/ percentages<br>● Speed/distance/time<br>● Area, perimeter and volume<br>● Ratio<br>● Proportion (direct/ indirect)<br>● Measurements |
| Statistics:<br>● Risk and probability<br>● Statistics in diagrams<br>● Analysing and comparing data sets<br>● Line of best fit | Measures:<br>● Calculating a quantity based on two related pieces of information<br>● Scale drawing<br>● Bearings and navigation<br>● Efficient container packing<br>● Precedence tables<br>● Time management<br>● Tolerance | Data:<br>● Extract/interpret data from three different formats<br>● Make/justify decisions using evidence from interpretation of data<br>● Make/justify decisions based on probability |
| Use reasoning skills and the skills above, linked to real-life contexts.<br><br>You will be asked to analyse, compare, justify and communicate. ◄——— The amount of reasoning is what makes Lifeskills Mathematics different. | | |

# Revision skills
## Good revision practice

- For revision to be really effective, you should begin by ensuring you are well organised. Good organisation begins long before exam day.
- Try to make sure you have a space dedicated to your revision. This space should have:
  - this *How To Pass National 5 Lifeskills Maths* book
  - class notes, summaries, jotters, worked examples
  - paper, pencil, ruler, rubber, protractor and a set of compasses
  - a scientific calculator (you should be familiar with its use)

  Collecting this material, and keeping it organised, will save you starting afresh each time you sit down to revise.
- Start revising in good time — don't leave it until the last minute.
- Work to a study plan: set up sessions and spread them out over several weeks. Make sure each session has a focus.
- Make sure you know exactly *when* each exam is. This seems obvious, but check with your teacher or the SQA website for day/date/times.
- Make sure you have a list of topics that are in the course — this will help you to study in chunks. When taking notes, try summarising each topic onto one sheet of A4.
- Make sure you know what to expect in the exam:
  - calculator and non-calculator papers
  - popular topics
  - number of marks in each paper
  - types of question
  - amount of time for each mark
- Practice, practice and more practice: there is no substitute for trying the real thing. A book of past papers is essential — these will give you practice in exam-style papers.
- Practise against the clock: begin by timing yourself for a number of marks (see the rough timings in the exam papers section below). Work up to doing a whole paper and checking against the time allowed.

- Study in a style that is comfortable for you:
  - V — visual — use diagrams, notes, symbols, charts and flashcards.
  - A — audio — listen to audio notes you have made, or get a family member to listen to you.
  - K — kinaesthetic — make posters or displays of your notes, showing connections between topics.
- Make full use of the school resources:
  - Are there after-school study classes? When can you ask your teacher for help?
  - Can you borrow study guides, past papers and textbooks?
- Look after your health. Take time to relax, keep hydrated (drink plenty of water), eat sensibly and get fresh air. All of these will help you to maintain concentration in the 'work cycle'.

## Bad revision practice

- Do *not* simply read through your notes/jotter/textbook without doing something *active*. Don't just look at examples — *do* them.
- Do *not* work where there are distractions. For example a television on in the room or friends waiting for you can be distracting and you will not work efficiently.
- Do *not* study for hours without a break. Work in small chunks. For example, work/study for about 30–45 minutes and then take a 10-minute break. Repeat this cycle a couple of times in the evening. When you take a break, get away from your study area, get some air, take a drink of water and clear your thoughts.
- Do *not* simply copy out notes — although this will look good on paper, there may not be much in the memory. Instead you may wish to consider putting your notes into a different format that makes you *think* about what you are doing. For example, you could make your notes into mind maps or spider diagrams, or condense them onto small cards for use during another revision session. You could make three piles for the topics you are studying — 'I can do this', 'I'm not sure' and 'Jings!' As your revision progresses, you move topics from the 'Jings!' pile to the 'I'm not sure pile', and so on, until you get more and more confident.

## Top five revision tips

- Have a revision mentality for the whole year — with clear notes, index cards etc.
- Use time carefully — start as early in the course as you can, use a revision timetable and work in short chunks.

- Stay positive — keep your motivation going and face challenges head on.
- Use previous/model exam papers — look at regular themes and wording.
- Use memory aids such as mind maps, notes and flashcards.

## Mind maps

Some students like to use mind maps to summarise notes on a topic. Here is an example of one:

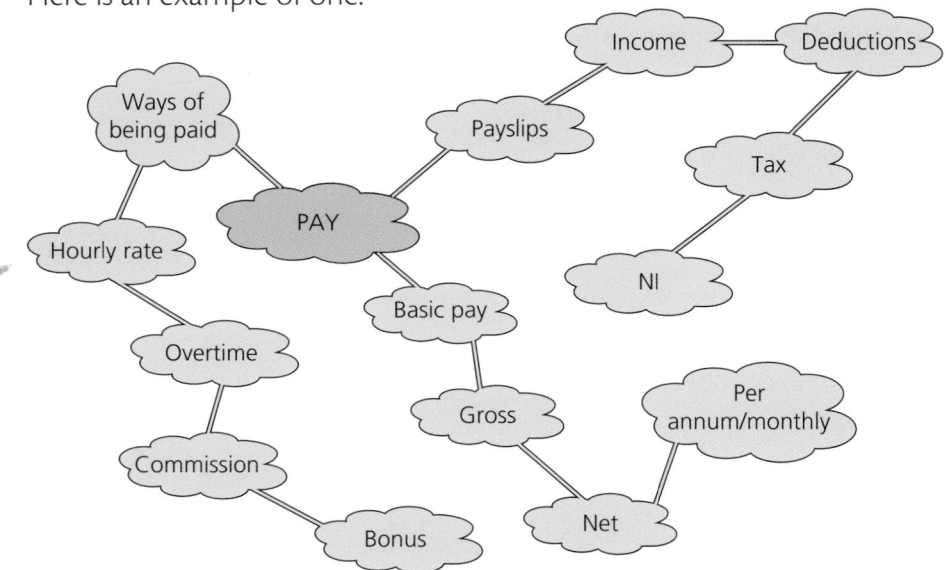

# The exam papers

You should be familiar with the examination papers — the timings, the marks, the types of question, the allocation of marks and whether a calculator is allowed or not. This knowledge helps you prepare and means that you will go into the exam with some confidence that nothing unexpected will occur.

For National 5 Lifeskills Mathematics the exam papers are as follows:
- Paper 1     Non-calculator       35 marks       50 minutes
- Paper 2     Calculator allowed     55 marks       1 hour 40 minutes

Paper 1 consists of a mixture of short, medium and extended questions, ranging from 2 to 6 marks. This paper covers a range of operational and reasoning skills. Short questions assess one operational/reasoning skill, while longer questions assess across different skills and units.

This allows you just under a minute and a half per mark — this should help you to pace yourself through the paper. For example, if a question is worth 5 marks you should spend no more than about 7 minutes on it.

Paper 2 consists of a series of case studies — a set of themed questions that look for more sustained focus when answering. Each case study consists of information and data along with a set of questions based on this information and data.

Again there are short, medium and extended case studies, ranging from 4 to around 15 marks.

The time allocated to this paper allows you reading and 'absorption' time, as there is quite a lot of information to digest, analyse, reason with, calculate and communicate.

This allows you just under 2 minutes per mark (about 1.8 minutes!) so if a question is worth, say, 10 marks you should allow about 18 minutes for it.

These timings are simply guides, but hopefully give you an idea of how to pace yourself through the examination.

# Improving your mark

The most important piece of advice is *show all your working clearly*.

The instructions on the exam paper state that 'Full credit will only be given where the solution contains appropriate wording'.

As far as possible use the Formula–Substitute–Calculate rule and set your working out neatly in a column, preferably with = signs lined up:

formula = (formula stated) ——— Formula

    = numbers substituted in the correct places ——— Substitute

    = answer calculated ——— Calculate

    = answer rounded if required, and *units used*

## Example

If John travels 200 miles at an average speed of 47 miles per hour, how long will it take him to complete his journey?

Give your answer to the nearest minute.

$$speed = \frac{distance}{time}$$

$$time = \frac{distance}{speed}$$ ——————— Formula

$$= \frac{200}{47}$$ ——————— Substitute

$$= 4.26 \text{ hours}$$ ——————— Calculate

$$= 4 \text{ hours } 15.6 \text{ minutes}$$

$$= 4 \text{ hours } 16 \text{ minutes to the nearest minute}$$ ——— Answer

This will allow the marker to follow your working clearly. It will also show that you know what to do. And when you have completed all your answers and are looking over your paper, it should be clear to you what you have done!

Remember that correct answers with no working might gain no marks (or only partial marks). However, an incomplete answer — which has some working — will gain marks for any appropriate working shown.

Never cross out working unless you are happy that you have replaced it with something better.

In Lifeskills Mathematics you will often be asked to *justify your answer* or *use your working to justify your answer*. To do this you must set your working out clearly – and then use it to *make a statement*. Don't just state the answer — make a comparison, statement or recommendation.

## Example

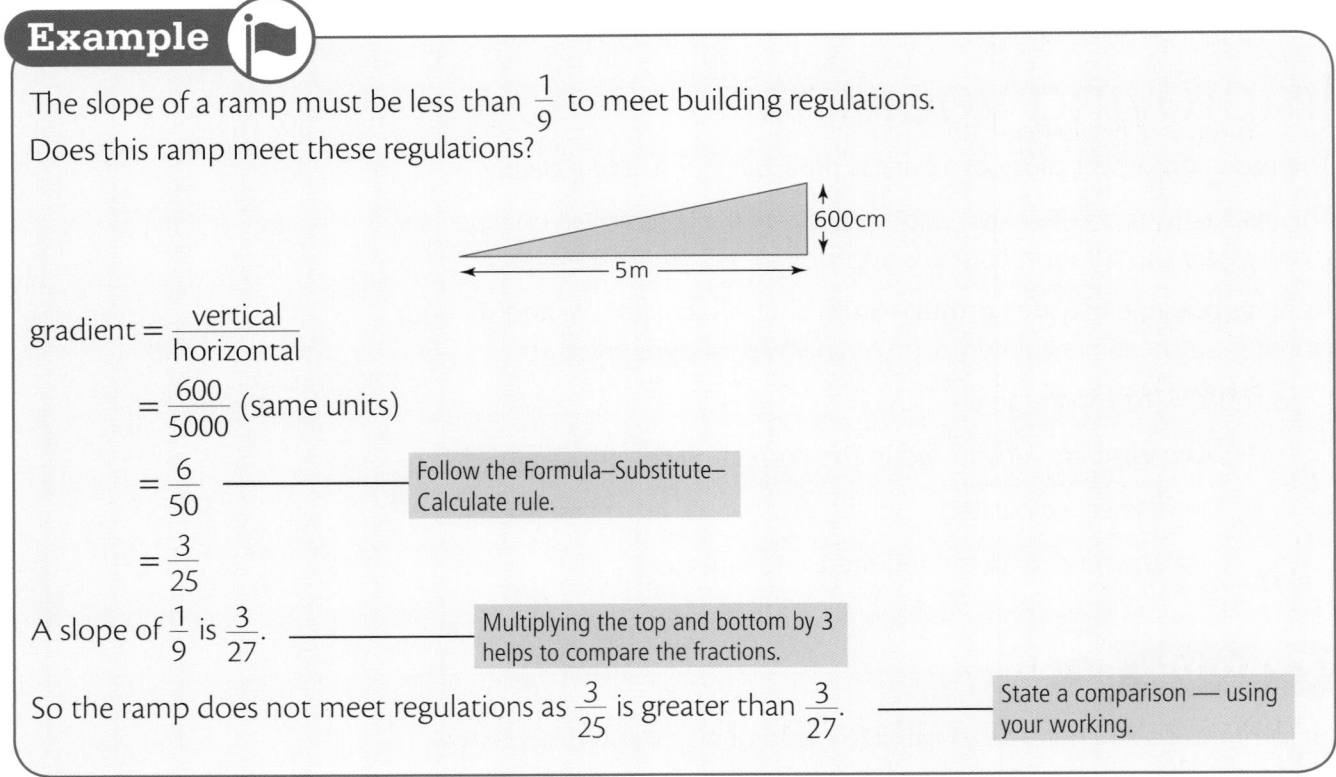

The slope of a ramp must be less than $\frac{1}{9}$ to meet building regulations. Does this ramp meet these regulations?

600 cm

5 m

$$\text{gradient} = \frac{\text{vertical}}{\text{horizontal}}$$

$$= \frac{600}{5000} \text{ (same units)}$$

$$= \frac{6}{50}$$      Follow the Formula–Substitute– Calculate rule.

$$= \frac{3}{25}$$

A slope of $\frac{1}{9}$ is $\frac{3}{27}$.      Multiplying the top and bottom by 3 helps to compare the fractions.

So the ramp does not meet regulations as $\frac{3}{25}$ is greater than $\frac{3}{27}$.      State a comparison — using your working.

*Always* attempt every question, even if you are not sure if you are on the right track. Your solution may contain working that will gain some marks. Remember that a blank piece of paper certainly will *not* gain any marks.

If a question has more than one part, and you are not sure of how to answer the first part, don't give up. You may be able to answer parts b and c – thus gaining valuable marks.

For each question think about what the main topic is — look for key words that will give you a clue. On your answer paper write down these ideas. This will help you to focus on the question. If you get stuck, move on; you can come back to it later and will have some ideas to prompt you.

The examination papers are designed so that, for most students, the questions will get slightly longer and harder as you work through the paper. So it may be an idea to work through the paper in order, so that you get 'warmed up' on the shorter, easier questions before tackling the longer ones, which will cover more than one skill or unit.

*Do not* leave the examination room before the end of the allotted time. If you think you have finished — and still have some time left — use this time to look through your answers. Check that you have used units, that the working is clearly set out and that you have answered *all* the questions. Look closely at any questions you did not finish to see if an idea springs to mind.

# Formulae list

Each paper will have the following formulae list:

Circumference of a circle    $2\pi r$ or $\pi d$

Area of a circle    $\pi r^2$

Volume of a cylinder    $\pi r^2 h$

Volume of a prism    $Ah$

Volume of a sphere    $\frac{4}{3}\pi r^3$

Volume of a cone    $\frac{1}{3}\pi r^2 h$

Theorem of Pythagoras    $c^2 = a^2 + b^2$

Standard deviation $s = \sqrt{\dfrac{\sum(x-\bar{x})^2}{n-1}}$  or $s = \sqrt{\dfrac{\sum x^2 - (\sum x)^2/n}{n-1}}$

Gradient $= \dfrac{\text{vertical height}}{\text{horizontal distance}}$

# What you should know
## Know your calculator

- Know how your calculator works — for example, does it use BODMAS?
- Know how to round answers.
- Have a rough idea of the *size* of answer expected before committing to paper.
- Check that you know how to get squares and square roots on your calculator.
- Check that you know how to calculate percentages on your calculator.
- Throughout this book, 3·14 is used as an approximate value for $\pi$. If you use the $\pi$ button on your calculator, your answers may be slightly different from those in the answers section of this book.

## Know your working

- In every question, show *clearly* how you arrive at an answer.
- Lifeskills, more than many other paper, emphasises *working*, as this shows your reasoning — which is the main focus of this exam.
- Marks are awarded for what is done correctly — so, obviously, no working = no marks.

- Never cross out working unless you have something better with which to replace it — and do not cross it out until you *have* replaced it.
- Try to set out all your working neatly and in a sequence that is easy to follow.
- Having lines of working set out in a nice column makes it easier to follow your train of thought — and it is also more difficult for the examiner to miss pieces of work you have used.

## Know your wording

- Read each question carefully.
- The first time is a read through to get a feel for the question.
- In the next read through you should underline/highlight key words — words with which you are familiar, and ones that give you a clue as to the topic.
- You can quickly jot down what you remember about this topic — this will often focus your mind, ready to formulate a more coherent answer.
- Often, by writing down these key words, your memory is triggered to recall when you practised these types of questions in class; and if you have practised regularly, the method will come to you.
- Remember that the examiner can only award marks if there is something there!

# Development of skills for learning, skills for life and skills for work

Success in this course will not only give you a certificate at National 5 level, but it should also help to equip you for further study and life after school.

It is expected that you will develop broad, generic skills that you can apply to other areas of the curriculum and to life and work.

Throughout this course you will have developed your skills in:
- Numeracy:
  - Number processes
  - Money, time and measurement
  - Information handling
- Thinking:
  - Applying
  - Analysing and evaluating

# Chapter 1

# Managing finance and statistics

## Unit requirements

This unit has two stated outcomes:

* Use reasoning skills and financial skills linked to real-life contexts.
* Use reasoning skills and statistical skills linked to real-life contexts.

Financial skills include:

* analysing a financial position using budget information
* analysing and interpreting factors affecting income
* determining the best deal (given three pieces of information)
* converting between several currencies (at least three currencies in a multi-stage task)
* investigating the impact of interest rates on savings and borrowing

Statistical skills include:

* using a combination of statistics to investigate risk and its impact on life
* using a combination of statistical information presented in different diagrams
* using statistics to analyse and compare data sets
* drawing a line of best fit from given data

# What kinds of question might you be asked?

## Finance section
Look for key words.

* You may be asked to complete a budget for a student moving into a flat.
* You may be asked to complete a payslip, or calculate pay for a week.
* You may be asked to work out how much tax someone should pay.
* You will investigate what is the best deal when various discounts are offered.
* You will convert between currencies as you travel from place to place.
* You may be asked to compare store cards, credit cards or purchase by, for example, hire purchase or credit agreement.

## Statistics section

* You may be asked about probability and expected frequency.
* You may need to draw or interpret statistics in a variety of diagrams, such as pie charts, multiple bar charts or line graphs.

- You may need to draw or interpret a box plot or scatter graph, including a line of best fit.
- You may need to calculate the standard deviation for a set of data and analyse what this means.

Later in this section we will look at some questions and how they should be answered. Remember that short questions will only ask about one topic but longer questions can involve two or three topics — and not all from the same section.

Remember that the questions in paper 1 are non-calculator, so you need to be able to work comfortably with numbers, including simple fractions and percentages. Questions in this paper vary from short (2–3 marks) to medium (3–5 marks) to extended (4–6 marks). Longer questions will probably be broken down into parts a, b and possibly c.

Paper 2 involves case studies varying from short (around 4 marks) to extended (up to around 15 marks). Remember that longer questions could involve topics from the other units, so in this case there could be some geometry and measures, or some numeracy and data, in the question.

Let us look at some typical questions for this unit.

# Section 1.1 Analysing a financial position using budget information

## What you should know

★ How to draw up a budget for a person.
★ How to calculate total income and total outgoings for a personal budget and stating whether the person has a surplus or deficit.
★ How to calculate what impact a change to one or more items has on the budget, how long it would take to save up to buy an item, or how long it would take before the purchase of an item 'pays for itself'.

## Key words

income, expenditure
surplus, deficit
incomings, outgoings
increase, decrease
balance

## Example

Cathy prepares a budget to check on her income and outgoings.

The spreadsheet below shows her monthly income and expenditure.

| Income | | Expenditure | |
|---|---|---|---|
| Pay | £1635 | Mortgage | £565 |
| | | Council tax | £235 |
| | | Food | £435 |
| | | Utilities | £235 |
| | | Car costs | £140 |

**a)** Does Cathy have a surplus or deficit, and by how much?

**b)** If Cathy's utilities rise by 11%, what impact will this have on her budget?

## Solution

Remember to look for key words. In this question these include *surplus* and *deficit* in part a), *rise, impact* and *budget* in part b).

When doing your exam you could underline these (or highlight them with a highlighter). This will keep you focused on exactly what the question is asking and how you should form your answer.

**a)** Add up expenditure:

$565 + 235 + 435 + 235 + 140 = 1610$ ———— Compare with income, which is more than 1610.

Cathy has a surplus of £25  $(1635 - 1610)$

**b)** Utilities increase by 11%:

10% of 235 = 23·50

1% of 235 = 2·35 ———— Use your number skills to calculate percentage.

11% = 25·85

Cathy now has a deficit of £0·85. ———— Make the answer relevant to the question.

# Section 1.2 Analysing and interpreting factors affecting income

## What you should know

- ★ How to calculate basic pay, overtime, gross pay and net pay.
- ★ How to calculate allowances and income tax.
- ★ How to calculate National Insurance and pension contributions.
- ★ How to calculate the elements of a payslip and complete a variety of payslips. ⇨

★ You may have to interpret job adverts/descriptions and to compare net pay for each — and make recommendations on which would be the better-paid job.

## Key words

basic pay, hourly rate
gross pay, net pay
deductions, National Insurance, income tax
bonus, commission
piecework, overtime
benefits and allowances
per annum

This topic may appear as a case study in paper 2.

## Example 1

Mary is paid £5·20 per hour.

For overtime she is paid at 'time and a half'.

How much will Mary get for 3 hours overtime?

### Solution

Key words: *per hour, time and a half, 3 hours overtime*

Get into the habit of underlining or highlighting these.

basic pay per hour = £5·20

    time and a half = £5·20 × 1·5 (or × 1½)

            = £7·80

     for 3 hours = £7·80 × 3

             = £23·40 ———— Set out working neatly.

Mary will get £23·40 for 3 hours overtime. ——— State your answer in context of the question.

## Example 2

Brian earns £21 040 per annum.

His allowances, before he has to pay tax, amount to £8800.

He pays tax at the basic rate of 20%.

How much tax does he pay each month?

## Solution

Key words: *per annum, allowances, tax at basic rate, each month*

taxable income = £21 040 − 8800

= £12 240 ——— Work it out per annum (per year).

tax is 20% of £12 240 = 1224 × 2 (10% × 2)

= £2448 pa

monthly tax = $\frac{£2448}{12}$ ——— The question asked each *month*.

= £204

Brian will pay £204 per month in income tax.

## Example 3

Julie joins a company at an annual gross pay of £18 750 per year. Her personal allowance is £8105 and she pays income tax at a rate of 20%. At the end of her first year, Julie is given a pay rise of 1·35%.

**a)** How much is her annual gross pay after the pay rise?
**b)** How much annual income tax does Julie pay after the pay rise?

## Solution

Key words: *gross pay, income tax, personal allowance, pay rise*

**a)** Gross pay:

new salary = £18 750 × 1·0135 ——— 100% = 1, 1·35% = 0·0135 so a rise of 1·35% requires a multiplier of 1·0135

= £19 003·13 (rounded to the nearest penny)

**b)** Income tax:

taxable pay = 19 003·13 − 8105

= £10 898·13

income tax at 20% = 20% of £10 898·13

= £2179·63 (rounded to the nearest penny)

## Example 4

The table shows the payments an employee would make towards his or her National Insurance contribution.

| Earnings | National Insurance | Formula |
|---|---|---|
| Up to £7592 | 0% | No NI contribution payable |
| Between £7592 and £42 484 | 12% | = (pay − 7592) × 0·12 |

Using this table, how much National Insurance would Julie (from Example 3 above) pay after her pay rise?

> pay after rise = £19 003 (to the nearest pound)
>
> amount on which NI contributions are charged = 19 003 − 7592
>
> $$= 11 411$$
>
> $$NI = 12\% \text{ of } £11 411$$
>
> $$= £1369·32$$

> This refers to the 2nd row of the table and is less than £42 484

# Section 1.3 Determining the best deal (given three pieces of information)

## What you should know

* ★ You will be expected to compare three different products. Each of the three products will have three pieces of information. For example, you may be asked to compare mobile phone tariffs covering minutes of calls, texts and data usage. Another example may be to compare companies offering services such as hiring equipment.
* ★ How to compare offers such as '3 for 2', or tariffs for, say, landline phones, TV/broadband packages, car-hire rates, holiday prices and other contexts such as these.
* ★ Questions involving this topic may also include graphs for you to interpret. For example, it may be better to go with one company up to a certain 'stage' and then with another company beyond that.

## Key words

compare
tariff, rate
cheaper, cheapest, most economical
unit costs

## Example 1

Three companies rent out motorbikes on a holiday island. The charges are set out below.

|  | Hire-a-Bike | Bike-4-U | We-R-Bikes |
|---|---|---|---|
| **125 cc** | 20p per mile | 22p per mile | 30p per mile |
| **250 cc** | 35p per mile | 40p per mile | 60p per mile |
| **500 cc** | 50p per mile | 52p per mile | 70p per mile |
| **Per day charge** | £15 per day | £13·50 per day | £12 per day |

Sam wants to hire a 250 cc bike for 10 days. He expects to travel 100 miles.

Which company should he choose? Use your working to justify your answer.

## Solution

The key words here would help you to choose which parts of the table you need to look at.

Look for the important information in the question:

- 250 cc — so look along that row
- 100 miles — so cost per mile × 100
- 10 days — look at the daily charge

Interpret the table to select correct row; note the cost per mile; note the cost per day; do the calculation for each; state the result.

Hire-a-Bike: 35p × 100 = £35

£15 × 10 = £150

total cost = £185

Bike-4-U: 40p × 100 = £40

£13·50 × 10 = £135

total cost = £175

We-R-Bikes: 60p × 100 = £60

£12 × 10 = £120

total cost = £180

Sam should choose Bike-4-U because it is the cheapest option: £175 < £180 < £185.

You would get no marks for simply stating 'Bike-4-U'. The question quite clearly states 'Use your working…'. When you state your answer, *give a reason*.

## Example 2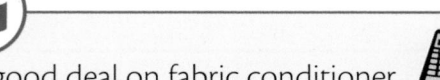

Grigor is looking for a good deal on fabric conditioner.

He sees the following adverts in the 'Homecare' aisle in a supermarket:

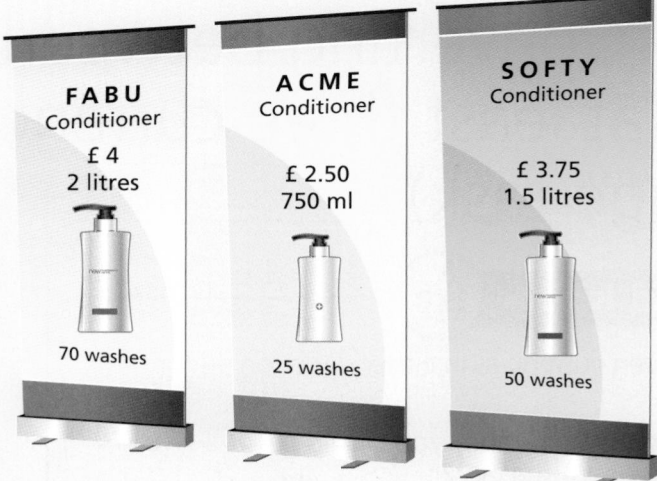

**a)** Which conditioner is best value per litre?
**b)** Which is best value per wash?
**c)** Which conditioner gives most washes per litre?
**d)** Which one would you recommend Grigor buys?

## Solution

**a)** Fabu: cost per litre $= \frac{£4}{2} = £2$ per litre

Acme: cost per litre $= \frac{£2·50}{0·75} = £3·33$ per litre

Softy: cost per litre $= \frac{£3·75}{1·5} = £2·50$ per litre

So Fabu is best value per litre as £2 per litre is the cheapest of the three. — You must lay out your working clearly.

**b)** Fabu: cost per wash $= \frac{£4}{70} = 5·71$p per wash

Acme: cost per wash $= \frac{£2·50}{25} = 10$p per wash

Softy: cost per wash $= \frac{£3·75}{50} = 7·5$p per wash

So Fabu is best value per wash as 5·71p per wash is cheapest option.

**c)** Fabu: washes per litre $= \frac{70}{2} = 35$ washes per litre

Acme: washes per litre $= \frac{25}{0·75} = 33·3$ washes per litre

Softy: washes per litre $= \frac{50}{1·5} = 33·3$ washes per litre

So Fabu is best value in terms of washes per litre.

**d)** Grigor should buy Fabu as it is best value in all three comparisons. — You would get no marks for simply stating Fabu (or any other one). When you state your answer, *give a reason.*

# Section 1.4 Converting between currencies (at least three currencies in multi-stage task)

## What you should know

★ How to convert between currencies in either direction — for example, from £s to €s.
★ How to calculate how much currency you would get at a given exchange rate, including commission if it is charged.
★ How to compare a higher exchange rate with commission against a lower exchange rate without commission.
★ You may also have to take into account charges if using an ATM abroad, and how this may compare with exchanging money before you depart.

## Key words

currency, exchange rates
commission, fees, charges, credit transaction costs
bureaux de change

A typical question may be about a family travelling to, say, France and Switzerland. This could involve changing £s to euros (€) for France, then Swiss francs (CHF), and then converting the remainder back into £s. If real exchange rates are used, this is more likely to be part of a case study in paper 2, where a calculator would be handy for converting from one currency to another.

## Example

Mike is travelling to France with his wife and two friends. They are flying to Geneva Airport, where they will hire a car.

Mike is paying for the car on his credit card, in Swiss francs (CHF).

(Geneva airport is in Switzerland, near the French border.)

The four travellers will share the cost of the car hire equally between them.

The cost of the car hire, in pounds, is £280.

The exchange rate of £s to Swiss francs is £1 = CHF1·44.

The exchange rate of Swiss francs to euros is CHF1 = €0·81.

How much should each of the other three pay Mike if he wants the money in euros?

### Solution

£280 in CHF = 280 × 1·44

$\qquad$ = CHF403·20

shared four ways = $\dfrac{\text{CHF403·20}}{4}$

$\qquad$ = CHF100·80 (so each person should pay CHF100·80)

convert to €s = 100·80 × 0·81

$\qquad$ = €81·65 (rounded)

So each person should give Mike €81·65 to cover their share of the cost of the hire car.

This would be typical of a shorter case study. To make it a medium or extended case study, the theme may also include flight times, moving across time zones, comparing costs of hotels and so on.

# Section 1.5 Investigating the impact of interest rates on savings and borrowing

## What you should know

★ You need to be familiar with methods of calculating interest — both simple and compound.
★ How to compare costs involved with credit cards, debit cards, credit agreements and store cards.
★ You may be asked to calculate costs of buying an item by different methods.
★ You should be familiar with terms such as HP, APR, interest rates, credit charge and per annum.

## Key words

loans, savings, borrowing, invest
credit cards, store cards, credit agreements
annual percentage rate (APR), annual equivalent rate (AER)
interest rates, credit charge, early repayment fees
simple interest, compound interest, return
per annum
principal, multiplier, term, balance

## Example 1

Rory invests £800 in a savings account.
The interest rate is 1·35% per annum.
How much interest will he earn after 5 months?

### Solution

Key words: *invest, interest rate, per annum*

1·35% of £800 = 1·35 × 8

$= £10·80$ — Calculate for 1 year (per annum).

5 months $= \left(\frac{5}{12}\right) \times 10·80$ — Calculate for the stated period.

$= £4·50$

Rory would receive £4·50 in interest after 5 months.

## Hints & tips

Remember:
• *write down the formula*
• *substitute the numbers*
• *calculate*
• *state the answer*

## Example 2

Kelvin has an antique valued at £400.

He reckons it will increase in value by 4·5% each year.

What will the antique be worth after 5 years?

### Solution

Use the formula:

amount = principal × multiplier$^{(years)}$

$\qquad$ = 400 × 1·045$^5$

$\qquad$ = £498·47

After 5 years the antique will be worth £498·47.

## Example 3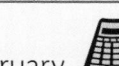

Duncan spends £320 on his credit card in February.

The credit card company charges interest at 1·5% per month.

Duncan must pay £5 or 3% of the balance, whichever is greater.

How much would he have to pay at the end of February?

How much interest would he be charged (on the balance)?

Duncan makes this minimum payment.

What would his opening balance be for March?

### Solution

3% of £320 = £9·60

This is more than £5 so Duncan must pay £9·60. ——— Compare and state your conclusion.

interest = 1·5% of (320 − 9·60)

$\qquad$ = £4·66

opening balance for March = 320 − 9·60 + 4·66 ——— Use your previous working.

$\qquad\qquad$ = £315·06

# Section 1.6 Using a combination of statistics to investigate risk and its impact on life

## What you should know

★ How to link simple probability with the expected frequency of an event.
★ How to link simple probability and risks, for example in relation to the life expectancy of smokers.

$\Rightarrow$

- ★ How to assess the efficiency of a medicine against the cost of administering it.
- ★ The effects of $CO_2$ emissions.
- ★ Road safety statistics.
- ★ Diet and the risk of cancer and similar scenarios.

## Key words

probability, event
frequency, expected frequency
likelihood, risk

## Example

Cigarette smoke contains 4800 chemicals, of which 69 contribute to the causes of cancer.

What is the probability that one of these chemicals taken at random is likely to be one that contributes towards cancer? Simplify the fraction.

### Solution

Key words: *probability, simplify*

$$\text{probability} = \frac{69}{4800}$$ ———— Divide the top and bottom by 3.

$$= \frac{23}{1600}$$

# Section 1.7 Using a combination of statistical information presented in different diagrams

## What you should know

- ★ You may be asked to look at tables of statistics and interpret them.
- ★ Diagrams such as line graphs, stem-and-leaf diagrams and bar charts could be given, and you will need to interpret them in some way.
- ★ You should also be able to interpret one graph/diagram and compare it with another form of statistical representation. For example, comparing a stem-and-leaf diagram with a box plot.
- ★ Identify overlaps while analysing and comparing data.

## Key words

diagrams, graphs, tables, charts
line, bar, stem-and-leaf, back to back, box plots, dot plots, pie charts
trend
range, quartiles, inter-quartile range
compare, contrast, recommend, justify

## Example 1

Dylan recorded the temperature in his greenhouse every
4 hours. His results are shown below.

| Time | 0000 | 0400 | 0800 | 1200 | 1600 | 2000 | 2400 |
|---|---|---|---|---|---|---|---|
| Temperature/°C | 5 | 4 | 8 | 20 | 23 | 15 | 7 |

Draw a line graph and estimate the temperature at 2 p.m. and
at 10 p.m.

If the electric windows open when the temperature exceeds
20°, for how long, during the day, will the windows be open?

## Solution

Construct suitable axes — horizontal should be time and
vertical should be temperature:

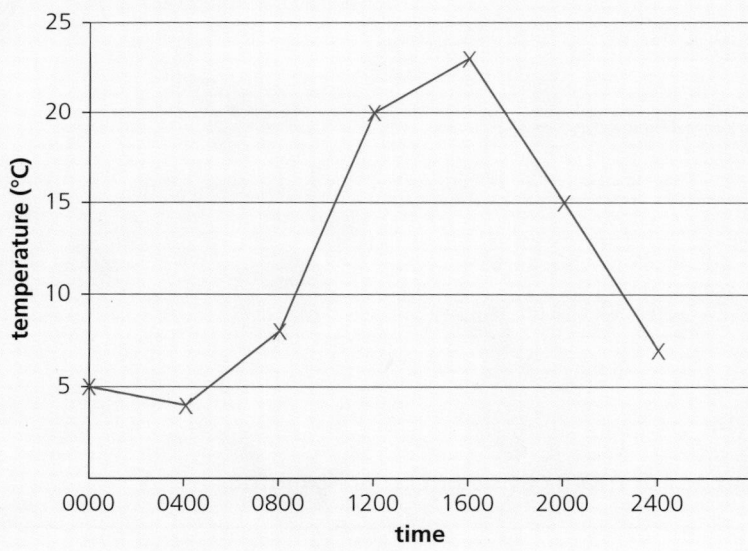
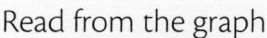

Read from the graph:

2 p.m. halfway between 1200 and 1600, so about 22°

10 p.m. halfway between 2000 and 2400, so about 11°

The windows will open at 20°, which is reached at 1200, and close at 1800 approximately.

So the windows will stay open for 6 hours.

## Example 2

Callum asked his friends how many text messages they sent in a day.

The data are shown below:

10  46  30  11  28  33  17  12  21  19

35  24  17  52  16  37  23  29  40  30

Rachael asked the same question of her friends.

She constructed a stem-and-leaf diagram to illustrate her data, as shown below:

| 1 | 1 | 4 | 5 |   |   |   |   |
|---|---|---|---|---|---|---|---|
| 2 | 1 | 2 | 4 | 6 | 6 | 8 | 9 |
| 3 | 2 | 5 | 5 | 6 | 7 | 7 |   |
| 4 | 0 | 3 | 8 |   |   |   |   |
| 5 | 5 |   |   |   |   |   |   |

$n = 20$
2|1 represents 21 texts.

**a)** Illustrate Callum's data on a box plot.

**b)** State the lower and upper quartiles for Rachael's data.

**c)** Compare the two inter-quartile ranges and make a valid statement about them.

## Solution

**a)** L = 10

Q1 = 17

Q2 = 26

Q3 = 34

H = 52 ——————— Write a five-figure summary (see Hints & tips, p. 15).

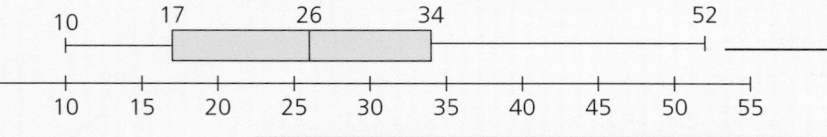

Transfer the figures to a box plot.

**b)** Q1 = 23 ——————— Halfway between 22 and 24 — the 5th and 6th numbers.

Q3 = 37

**c)** Callum's inter-quartile range is 34 − 17 = 17.

Rachael's inter-quartile range is 37 − 23 = 14.

So the data for Rachael are slightly less spread (or more consistent) than Callum's.

## Hints & tips ⭐

*If asked to draw a box plot, you need to construct something like this:*

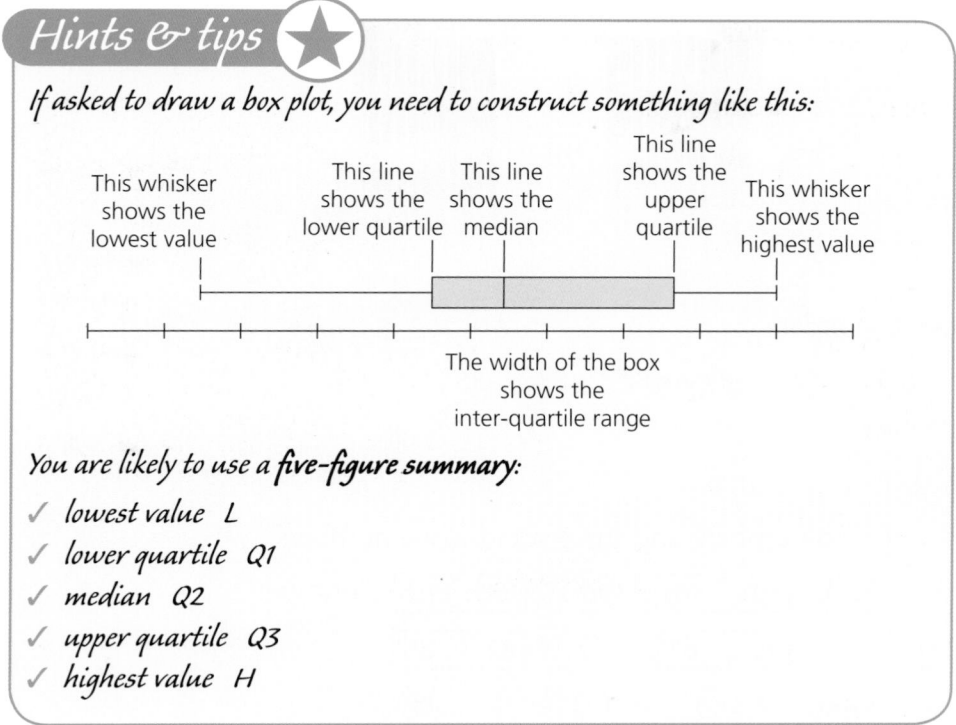

*You are likely to use a **five-figure summary**:*

- ✓ *lowest value   L*
- ✓ *lower quartile   Q1*
- ✓ *median   Q2*
- ✓ *upper quartile   Q3*
- ✓ *highest value   H*

# Section 1.8 Using statistics to analyse and compare data sets

## What you should know

- ★ How to draw, interpret and compare data sets in formats such as box plots, scatter graphs, stem-and-leaf diagrams and pie charts.
- ★ How to calculate and use mean, median, range, inter-quartile range and standard deviation.

## Key words

interpret, compare, analyse,
state, draw, construct
graph, chart, diagram
box plot, scatter diagram, stem-and-leaf, back-to-back stem-and-leaf, pie chart
mean, median, mode
range, inter-quartile range, quartiles,
spread, consistent, varied
standard deviation

## Example 1

Here is a set of scores from a golfing competition:

76    79    76    74    75    71    85    82    82    79    81

Draw a box plot for the set of scores.

### Solution

First re-write the scores in ascending order.

71    74    75    76    76    79    79    81    82    82    85

Construct your five-figure summary.

Note that there are 11 scores.

$\frac{11}{4} = 2$ r. 3, so four boxes each with two numbers, and three stand-alone numbers:

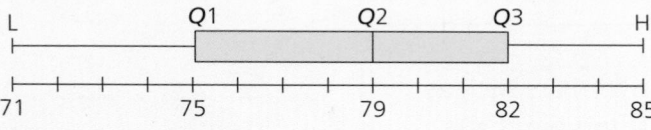

L = 71

Q1 = 75

Q2 = 79

Q3 = 82

H = 85

Now put these into a box plot. Remember to write in 'scale' and label all five points.

A typical extension to this type of question would be to ask you to make a comparison with another box plot, or possibly another statistical diagram.

(See Example 2 on p. 14 comparing a box plot and a stem-and-leaf diagram.)

## Example 2

Mark sat six assessments in modern studies.

His marks, out of 15, were:

  6, 8, 9, 9, 11, 14

Tyrone sat the same tests. His mean was 10 and his standard deviation was 2·5.

**a)** Calculate the mean and standard deviation for Mark's data.
**b)** Make two valid statements to compare Mark and Tyrone's scores.

## Solution

**a)** Calculate the mean:

$$\text{mean} = \frac{\text{total}}{\text{number}}$$

$$= \frac{57}{6}$$

$$\bar{x} = 9\cdot5$$

Set up a table:

| $x$ | $\bar{x}$ | $x - \bar{x}$ | $(x - \bar{x})^2$ |
|---|---|---|---|
| 6 | 9·5 | −3·5 | 12·25 |
| 8 | 9·5 | −1·5 | 2·25 |
| 9 | 9·5 | −0·5 | 0·25 |
| 9 | 9·5 | −0·5 | 0·25 |
| 11 | 9·5 | 1·5 | 2·25 |
| 14 | 9·5 | 4·5 | 20·25 |
| | | | $\Sigma(x - \bar{x})^2 = 37\cdot5$ |

A table is a clear way of setting out the data.

Use the standard deviation formula:

$$s = \sqrt{\frac{\Sigma(x-\bar{x})^2}{n-1}}$$

$$= \sqrt{\frac{37\cdot5}{5}} \quad (5 \text{ is } 6 - 1)$$

$$= \sqrt{7\cdot5}$$

$$= 2\cdot74 \text{ to 2 decimal places}$$

Remember: Formula–Substitute–Calculate.

So Mark has a mean score of 9·5; sd = 2·74.

**b)** Tyrone has a mean score of 10; sd = 2·5.

So, on average, Tyrone has slightly better scores (the mean is higher) and his scores are more consistent (sd 2·5 < 2·74, so less spread out).

## Hints & tips

Standard deviation is a more reliable measure of spread because it includes all the data in the calculation, rather than, say, two if looking at inter-quartile range. It measures the average deviation (or difference) of each piece of data from the mean.

The larger the value of the standard deviation, the larger the spread of the data from the mean.

# Section 1.9 Drawing a line of best fit from given data

## What you should know

★ The difference here between N4 and N5 is that you are likely to be asked to compare lines of best fit, or to use your line of best fit to decide on a likely result.

## Key words

line of best fit, best fitting line
compare, extend, estimate
relationship, correlation

## Example

a) Using the information in the table below, is there a relationship between the amount of fat in a food and the calories it contains?
b) If there is, how many calories would you expect to find in food containing 26 g of fat?

| Sandwich | Total fat/g | Total calories |
| --- | --- | --- |
| Hamburger | 9 | 260 |
| Cheeseburger | 13 | 320 |
| Quarter pounder | 21 | 420 |
| Quarter pounder with cheese | 30 | 530 |
| Big Mac | 31 | 560 |
| Arch sandwich special | 31 | 550 |
| Arch special with bacon | 34 | 590 |
| Crispy chicken | 25 | 500 |
| Fish fillet | 28 | 560 |
| Grilled chicken | 20 | 440 |
| Grilled chicken light | 5 | 300 |

## Solution

Construct a graph — horizontal axis is fat in g; vertical axis is calories.
Plot the points accurately. ⇒

Draw a line of best fit — try to get the 'slope' correct and have about the same number of points above as below the line.

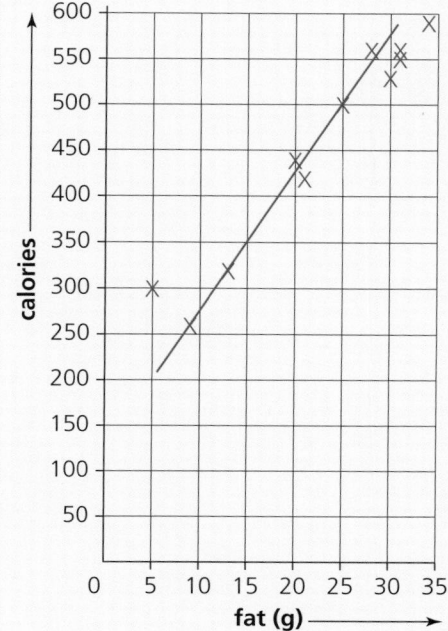

**a)** From the graph there appears to be a positive correlation. So yes, there is a connection between the amount of fat and the calories the food contains.

**b)** In food containing 26 g of fat you would expect around 510 calories.

## Practice questions

Here are a few questions for you to practise on your own. Mostly they are non-calculator but if a calculator is required this will be indicated in the question.

(The answers to the questions are given in Appendix 1.)

1   Grant works in a hospital. His basic pay is £8·20 per hour for a
    40-hour week.
    Overtime rates are:
    ○ time-and-a-half for weekday evenings (8 p.m.–12 midnight)
    ○ double time for weekends
    What would Grant's gross pay be for a week in which he works his basic
    40-hour week plus:
    ○ Wednesday 8 p.m.–10 p.m.
    ○ Thursday 8 p.m.–11 p.m.
    ○ Sunday 1 p.m.–5 p.m.

2  Ella has a pay-as-you-go phone and buys a voucher for £10. She pays the following rates:
   - Texts — 10p per text
   - Off-peak — 10p per minute
   - Peak — 30p per minute

   She makes 50 text messages, 15 minutes of off-peak calls and 10 minutes of peak-time calls.
   a) What balance will she have left?
   b) If the company raises the costs of texts to 12p per text, what effect would this have?

3  Rachel buys costume jewellery rings at £87·50 for 50. She sells them at a Saturday market for £2·45 each
   What percentage profit does she make?

4  Mike invests £700 in a savings account. He gets 1·2% per annum interest. How much interest will Mike earn after 7 months?

5  The table below shows the marks (%) scored by pupils in their biology and chemistry exams.

| Pupil | A | B | C | D | E | F | G | H |
|---|---|---|---|---|---|---|---|---|
| Biology | 22 | 56 | 17 | 87 | 46 | 77 | 42 | 92 |
| Chemistry | 27 | 63 | 12 | 79 | 58 | 69 | 64 | 87 |

   a) Draw a scatter diagram to illustrate these data.
   b) Mark in a line of best fit.
   c) A student missed the chemistry exam but scored 73% in biology. Use your line of best fit to estimate her chemistry mark.

6  Ninety people were asked which newspaper they read.
   - 45 read the *Daily Bugle*.
   - 20 read *Scotland Today*.
   - 15 read another paper.
   - 10 do not read a paper.
   a) Draw a pie chart to represent these data.
   b) What is the probability that a person chosen at random reads *Scotland Today*?

7  Patrick is paid 15% commission on all sales over £2000.
   What will his commission be if his sales amount to £4500?

8  A maths test is marked out of 50. The marks for the class are shown below:
   7, 36, 41, 39, 27, 21
   24, 17, 24, 31, 17, 13
   31, 19, 8, 10, 14, 45
   49, 50, 45, 32, 25, 17
   46, 36, 23, 18, 12, 6
   a) Draw a stem-and-leaf diagram to illustrate these data.
   b) Write down the median and lower and upper quartiles.
   c) Construct a box plot to illustrate these data.

9  Mary is selling tickets for a tombola at a local fete. She sells 100 tickets, numbered from 1 to 100. A prize is won if the number on the ticket ends in a 0 or a 5. What is the probability of drawing a winning ticket?

10  Bill and Ted are playing darts.
    Bill's scores are:

    72    71    68    72    69    71    73    72

    Ted's scores have a mean of 73 and a standard deviation of 2·1.
    a)  Calculate the mean and standard deviation of Bill's scores.
    b)  Write down two valid comparisons between Bill's scores and Ted's scores.

11  Katrina bought a car for £13 000.
    It depreciated in value at a rate of 12% per annum.
    Katrina hoped to sell it, after 4 years, for £9000.
    Was she being realistic in her expectations?

12  In a laboratory experiment, bacteria were increasing at a rate of 8% per hour.
    If there were 120 000 bacteria at the start of the experiment at 09·00, how many would there be at 2 pm? Give your answer to 2 significant figures.

13  A sports equipment company was developing a new 'step machine'.
    They developed five prototypes to try out in a sports centre.
    Customers at the sports centre were asked to try out the five prototypes and identify which one they preferred.
    The results are shown in the table below:

| Step type | Number of customers who preferred it |
|-----------|--------------------------------------|
| 'Step Up' | 28 |
| 'Step Along' | 14 |
| 'Side Step' | 6 |
| 'Double Step' | 22 |
| 'Quick Step' | 10 |

    Illustrate this information in an appropriate statistical diagram.

14  Six waiters in a restaurant had tips one week of:

    £35    £42    £80    £42    £37    £42

    a)  Calculate the mean, the median and the mode for this data set.
    b)  Which measure of 'average' would you choose to represent these data, and why?

# Chapter 2
# Geometry and measures

## Unit requirements

This unit has two stated outcomes:

* Use reasoning skills and geometric skills linked to real-life contexts.
* Use reasoning skills and measurement skills linked to real-life contexts.

Geometric skills include:

* investigating a situation involving gradient
* solving a problem involving the area of a composite shape, which could include part of a circle
* solving a problem involving the volume of a composite solid
* using Pythagoras' theorem within a two-stage calculation

Measurement skills include:

* calculating a quantity based on two related pieces of information
* constructing a scale drawing, including choosing a suitable scale
* planning a navigation course
* carrying out efficient container packing
* using precedence tables to plan a task
* solving a problem involving time management
* considering the effects of tolerance

# What kinds of question might you be asked?

## Geometry section

* You may be asked to calculate the slope or gradient of, say, a ramp, and determine if it meets certain requirements — for example, a slope of less than 1 in 12.
* You may be asked to work out the area of composite shapes — for example, an area to be tiled, or the area of an athletics field.
* You may be asked to work out the volume of a basic solid — for example, a cylinder or a sphere — and compare this with another solid (linked to the numeracy section).
* You may be asked to work out the volume of a composite solid — for example, a cylinder with a hemisphere on top, or a cuboid with a pyramid on top.
* You may be required to use Pythagoras' theorem to solve a problem where you need to apply the theorem twice — for example, to calculate a 'space diagonal' in a cuboid.

# Measures section

- You may be asked to calculate quantities that are in proportion based on two related pieces of information.
- You may be asked to construct a scale drawing for a given situation — for example, a garden plan.
- You may be asked to plan a navigation course — for example, an orienteering course.
- You will investigate the most efficient way to pack goods into a container, given dimensions.
- You will construct a precedence table to determine the maximum (and optimum) time required to complete a task, when some parts can be done simultaneously and others in sequence.
- You will be asked to solve a problem involving time management — for example, involving speed, distance and time, and across time zones.
- You may be asked to calculate acceptable limits of size when given a tolerance and to consider the implications if items do not match up to tolerance limits.

Later in this section we will look at some questions and how they should be answered. Remember that short questions will only ask about one topic but longer questions can involve two or three topics — and not all from the same section.

In the geometry section:
- you may need to work with fractions (for example, with gradients)
- area and volume overlap with numeracy
- you need to round to significant figures.

In the measures section:
- you may be asked about interpreting measurements (from numeracy)
- you may need to use or apply decimals, fractions and percentage calculations
- you could be asked to use speed, distance and time calculations to justify measurements
- you might need to calculate scale (using ratio).

In each of the above there may also be scope for topics from 'Managing finance and statistics' to be involved — for example, calculating costs, budgeting, best deal and statistics.

Remember that the questions in paper 1 are non-calculator, so you need to be able to work comfortably with numbers, including simple fractions and percentages. Questions in this paper vary from short (2–3 marks) to medium (3–5 marks) to extended (4–6 marks). Longer questions will probably be broken down into parts a, b and possibly c.

Paper 2 involves case studies varying from short (around 4 marks) to extended (up to around 15 marks). Remember that longer questions could involve topics from the other units — that is, there may be some finance and statistics or some numeracy and data in the question.

Let us look at some typical questions for this unit.

# Section 2.1 Calculate a quantity based on two related pieces of information

## What you should know

- ★ How to calculate direct proportion.
- ★ How to calculate inverse proportion.
- ★ How to calculate the connection between two measures such as pressure and temperature.
- ★ How to relate, for example, density, mass and volume.
- ★ How to calculate speed, distance or time, given the other two.
- ★ You may need to be able to overlap with best deal type questions.
- ★ You should be able to work comfortably with tables, charts and graphs.

## Key words

proportion (ratio), relationship
investigate
compare, justify and recommend

## Example 1

It takes Sunita 2 minutes to fill $\frac{4}{7}$ of the fuel tank in her car.

How long would it take to completely fill the tank?

### Solution

Key words: *minutes to, how long* (indicating proportion)

Set up a table:

| Tank | Time (min) |
|---|---|
| $\frac{4}{7}$ | 2 |
| 1 | $2 \times \dfrac{1}{\frac{4}{7}}$ |
| | $= 2 \times \dfrac{7}{4}$ |
| | $= \dfrac{14}{4}$ |
| | $= 3\frac{1}{2}$ minutes |

> More time will be needed, so expect a bigger answer and therefore the bigger number goes on top.
>
> Note that this question also involves numeracy by using fractions.

## Example 2

Rachel knows that if she travels at 70 miles per hour along the motorway, her journey will take her 2 hours 15 minutes. Due to roadworks the speed limit is reduced to 50 miles per hour.

How much longer will Rachel's journey take?

### Solution

Set up a table:

| Speed (mph) | Time (hours) |
|---|---|
| 70 | 2·25 |
| 50 | $2·25 \times \dfrac{70}{50}$ |
| | $= 3·15$ |
| | $= 3$ hours 9 minutes |

> More time will be needed, so expect a bigger answer and therefore the bigger number goes on top.

Rachel's journey will take 54 minutes longer. ———— Answer the question.

## Example 3

An office usually has six cleaners, who can clean the office in 2 hours.

The cleaners usually start at 6 am so that they are finished by 8 am.

One day a cleaner is absent.

When should the remaining cleaners start cleaning in order to be finished by 8 am?

### Solution

Start by finding how long it will take the five remaining cleaners.

Set up a table:

| Cleaners | Time (hours) |
|---|---|
| 6 | 2 |
| 5 | $2 \times \dfrac{6}{5}$ |
| | $= 2·4$ hours |
| | $= 2$ hours and 24 minutes |

> Fewer cleaners will take more time, so expect a bigger answer and therefore the bigger number goes on top.

> Change to hours and minutes.

So the cleaners would have to start 24 minutes earlier than usual.

The cleaners should start at 5.36 am. —————— Answer the question!

## Example 4

In science you may have learned that the resistance, $R$ (ohms), of  a given length of wire is inversely proportional to the *square* of its diameter, $d$ (mm).

For a wire of diameter 1 mm, the resistance is 8 ohms ($\Omega$).

**a)** Write the relationship in terms of $k = Rd^2$, where $k$ is a constant.
**b)** Calculate the resistance, $R$ (ohms), of a wire with diameter 1·5 mm.
**c)** What diameter of wire would have a resistance of 10 ohms?

## Solution

**a)** $k = Rd^2$

$\quad = 8 \times 1^2$

$\quad = 8$

So

$8 = Rd^2$

Or

$Rd^2 = 8$ ——————————— This is a formula that you can now use to answer other, connected, questions.

**b)** If $d = 1·5$ then:

$\quad Rd^2 = 8$

$R \times 1·5^2 = 8$

$R \times 2·25 = 8$

$\quad R = \dfrac{8}{2·25}$

$\quad R = 3·56 \text{ ohms}$

The resistance will be 3·56 ohms.

**c)** If $R = 10$ then:

$Rd^2 = 8$

$10 \times d^2 = 8$

$\quad d^2 = \dfrac{8}{10}$

$\quad\quad = 0·8$

$\quad d = \sqrt{0·8}$

$\quad\quad = 0·89$

The diameter will be 0·89 mm.

## Example 5

In rowing events, rowers have to decide how many strokes they take each minute.

The more strokes they make in a minute, the faster they will go — but they will also get tired more quickly.

**a)** In a practice row, Ben takes 198 strokes in 5 minutes 30 seconds. Calculate his strokes per minute rate.

**b)** If he continued this rate for a further 2 minutes, how many strokes would he have taken in total?

**c)** In another row, Ben 'upped' his rate to 40 strokes per minute. How long would he have taken to complete 270 strokes?

### Solution

**a)** Set up a table.

| Time (mins) | Strokes |
|---|---|
| 5·5 | 198 |
| 1 | Less, so $198 \times \dfrac{1}{5 \cdot 5}$ <br> = 36 strokes per minute |

> Expect a smaller answer and therefore the smaller number goes on top.

**b)** In 2 minutes he would take $36 \times 2 = 72$ more strokes. So:

$$\text{total} = 198 + 72$$

$$= 270 \text{ strokes}$$

**c)** 40 strokes per minute to cover 270 strokes $= \dfrac{270}{40}$

$$= 6 \cdot 75 \text{ minutes}$$

$$= 6 \text{ minutes and } 45 \text{ seconds}$$

# Section 2.2 Construct a scale drawing

## What you should know

★ You should be comfortable working with different scales and working with representative fractions and scale drawings.

★ How to apply scale to enlarge and reduce.

★ How to calculate a scale factor.

★ How to calculate real sizes from scale drawings or vice versa.

★ You may be asked to choose a suitable scale so that a drawing will fit to a given size.

★ You may be asked to use your calculations from a scale drawing to see if certain conditions are met — for example, if a slope of a ramp is too steep.

## Key words

scale, scale factor, scale drawing
representative fraction, maps and plans
enlarge and reduce
scale up and scale down

## Example 1

The distance from Edinburgh to Brechin, 'as the crow flies', is 180 kilometres.

How far apart would the two cities be on a map with a scale of 1:750 000?

### Solution

Key words: *on a map* (indicates use of scale)

The distance on the map will be measured in cm, so change 180 km to cm:

$180 \times 1000 \times 100 = 18\,000\,000$ cm ————— Keep units consistent.

Going from real to plan, so divide by the scale factor: ————— Think — big to small or small to big?

$$\frac{18\,000\,000}{750\,000} = 24$$

So the two cities are 24 cm apart on the map.

## Example 2

Karen and Jim want to put a fence around their garden. The measurements are shown in the diagram.

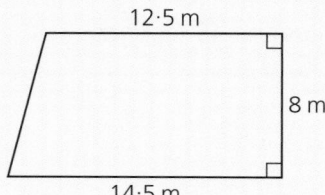

a) Use a scale of 1:200 to make a scale drawing of the garden.
b) Use your drawing to calculate the length of the sloping edge.
c) Fencing costs £15 per metre of length. Only whole numbers of metres may be purchased. How much will the fence cost?

### Solution

a) Calculate the scale lengths for the drawing by dividing by 200:

- 8 m = 800 cm  ÷ 200  line will be 4 cm long on drawing
- 12·5 m = 1250 cm  line will be 6·25 cm long on drawing
- 14·5 m = 1450 cm  line will be 7·25 cm long on drawing

$\Rightarrow$

These will be the measurements you use for your drawing.
Make a neat and accurate drawing.

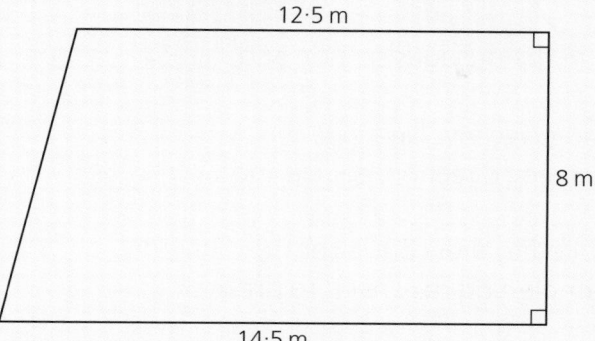

12·5 m

8 m

14·5 m

**b)** Measure the sloping edge.

Sloping edge is 4·1 cm.

So the real length is:

4·1 × 200 = 820 cm

= 8·2 m

**c)** total length of fencing = 8·2 + 8 + 14·5 + 12·5

= 43·2 m

Length of fence to be bought is 44 m (only whole number of metres).

cost = 44 × £15

= £660

## Example 3

A model car is 300 mm long and 120 mm high.

The real car is 4·5 m long.

**a)** Calculate the scale used in making the model car.
**b)** Use your answer to calculate the height of the real car.

## Solution

Key words: *scale, model*

**a)** Compare corresponding dimensions:

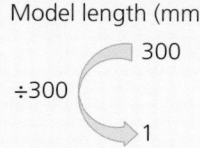

Model length (mm)          Real length (mm)

300          4500          ⎯⎯⎯⎯⎯⎯⎯⎯⎯ Convert to the same units.

÷300          ÷300

1          15

So the scale used is 1 to 15.

**b)** model height = 120

real height = 120 × 15 ⎯⎯⎯⎯ Use your answer.          Answer in appropriate units.
Remember, even if your
answer is wrong, you can
still get marks for following
through the calculation.

= 1800 mm

= 1·8 metres high ⎯⎯⎯⎯⎯⎯⎯⎯

# Section 2.3 Construct a navigation course

## What you should know

* ★ This follows on from your use of scale in the previous section and applies it to slightly different contexts.
* ★ You will need to be familiar with the language involved in navigation — for example, bearings, degrees, direction, course and compass points.
* ★ From a starting point you may be required to draw out a course, given distances and directions. For example, you may need to draw a short orienteering course.
* ★ You may also be asked to calculate distances and directions/ bearings from drawings.
* ★ You may be asked what direction and distance to go in order to get back to a starting point.
* ★ You may need to work out an efficient route around a set of points.
* ★ You may be asked to calculate how long a journey will take.

## Key words

bearings, direction, angle, degrees
distance, route, checkpoint

## Example 1

Donald is flying his hang-glider around three hills, as shown.

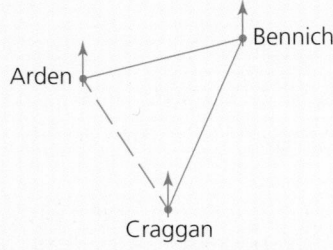

From Arden he flies for 2 km on a bearing of 075° to Bennich.

He then turns and flies to Craggan, a distance of 4 km on a bearing of 200°.

**a)** Use a scale 1:50 000 to make an accurate drawing of Donald's route. ——— Draw accurately and measure carefully.

**b)** What bearing should he follow to get back to Arden?

**c)** How far would this part of the flight be?

## ⇨ Solution

**a)** Steps to take:

- Mark in start point A and north arrow:

- Measure the angle (75°) and draw a line 4 cm long ——————

> 2 km = 200 000 cm
> ÷ 50 000 (scale factor) = 4 cm

- Mark in point B and north arrow.
- Continue until the diagram is completed.

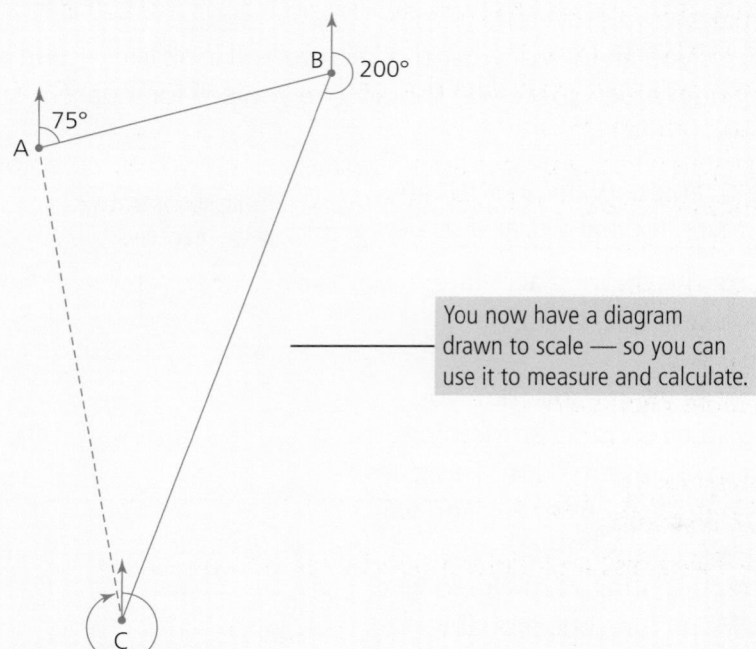

> You now have a diagram drawn to scale — so you can use it to measure and calculate.

**b)** The bearing from Craggan to Arden is 350° (use your protractor).

**c)** The distance is (measure on diagram) 6·6 cm × the scale factor to get the actual distance:

6·6 × 50 000 = 330 000 cm

= 3·3 km ——————

> In this example you drew the route yourself but you were given the scale to work to. Sometimes you may have to choose a suitable scale so that your drawing will fit to a given size.

## Example 2

Four dinghies are competing in a stage of a sailing race.

- Dinghy B is 7·6 km due east of dinghy A.
- Dinghy C is 9 km from dinghy A on a bearing of 210°.
- Dinghy D is due south of dinghy B.
- Dinghy D is on a bearing of 080° from dinghy C.

**a)** Use a suitable scale to draw the situation in the race.

**b)** Use your drawing to state how far and in what direction dinghy A is from dinghy D.

### Solution

**a)** First make a rough sketch.
This gives you an idea of what the 'picture' will look like — and an idea of how much space you should give yourself for a decent-sized drawing.

Mark in dinghy A and a north line. Then mark in dinghy B, and so on.

Remember: measure twice, draw once!

To make the drawing accurate, and a decent size, choose a suitable scale.
For sizes of 7·6 km and 9 km you may wish to consider something like 1 cm represents 1 km. This gives scale lengths of 7·6 cm etc. and will fit easily on an A4 sheet.
1 cm representing 2 km would give a smaller picture, but probably still large enough to take accurate measurements.

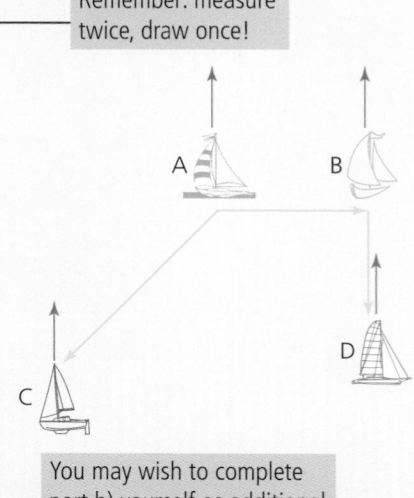

You may wish to complete part b) yourself as additional practice.

# Section 2.4 Carry out efficient container packing

## What you should know

★ How to fit items into uniform containers to minimise the number of containers required, and also to fit the items with a minimum of wasted space. This follows on from the 'first fit' method you may have met in N4 Lifeskills Mathematics.

★ Questions may involve exploring different ways to store items on a shelf, or how to fit cylinders into a cuboid case.

★ This topic may appear as part of a case study in paper 2.

## Key words

packing, fitting
efficient use of space
maximum, minimum
explore, investigate, recommend

## Example 1

CM Biscuits come in cuboid packets that are 22 cm long with an 8 cm square base, as shown.

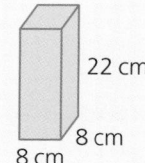

22 cm

8 cm

8 cm

They are to be packed in boxes, for taking to the supermarket, which are 44 cm long by 32 cm wide by 24 cm high.

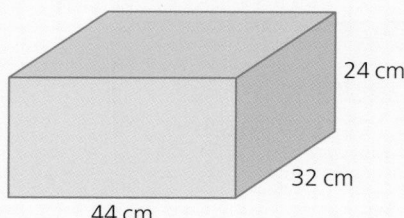

24 cm

32 cm

44 cm

Explain the different ways in which the packets can be packed into boxes and recommend the method that allows most packets to be packed and which wastes the least space.

## Solution

### Method A

Matching length 22 cm with 44, breadth 8 cm with 32 and height 8 cm with 24 gives:

2 packets × 4 packets × 3 packets = 24 packets

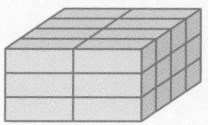

### Method B

Matching length 22 cm with 32, breadth 8 cm with 44 and height 8 cm with 24 gives:

1 × 5 × 3 = 15 packets

But you could get two more cross-wise in three rows, giving 21:

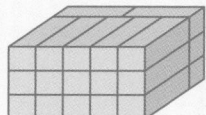

## Method C

Stack the packets upright.

So 24 cm would allow 1 packet vertical (not enough space to put one on top).

8 cm with 44 gives 5 packets, and 8 cm with 32 gives 4 packets:

$1 \times 5 \times 4 = 20$ packets

So method A is best — giving most packets, and also therefore wasting least space.

## Example 2

The Rent-a-Van-and-a-Man Company uses its van to deliver 'white goods' (fridges, washing machines, dishwashers etc.) to customers.

The company's van has dimensions of:

- length       2·4 m
- breadth     1·25 m
- height       1·5 m

The weight limit of a load is 460 kilograms.

White goods cannot be stacked one on top of the other.

Jenny and Tom run the 'Dunroamin' bed and breakfast.

They want two fridges, three washing machines and two dishwashers delivered.

The dimensions of each is shown below.

| Machine | Height (mm) | Width (mm) | Depth (mm) | Weight (kg) |
|---|---|---|---|---|
| Fridge | 870 | 600 | 560 | 45 |
| Washing machine | 890 | 640 | 580 | 75 |
| Dishwasher | 890 | 600 | 580 | 72 |

Can Rent-a-Van-and-a-Man do this in one trip, without breaking regulations? If so, show how the goods could be packed in the van.

## Solution

Check for weight:

$$2 \text{ fridges} = 2 \times 45 = 90 \text{ kg}$$

$$3 \text{ washing machines} = 3 \times 75 = 225 \text{ kg}$$

2 dishwashers $= 2 \times 72 = 144\,\text{kg}$

Total weight of load $= 459\,\text{kg}$

Since $459 < 460$, the weight of the load is within the acceptable limit.

Now we need to check if the goods will fit without being stacked up.

floor space $= 2{\cdot}4\,\text{m} \times 1{\cdot}25\,\text{m} = 2400\,\text{mm} \times 1250\,\text{mm}$

Use a sketch — consider making scale drawings of the white goods and trying different ways to fit them.

| Fridge 600 × 560 | Fridge 600 × 560 | Dishwasher 600 × 580 | Dishwasher 600 × 580 |
|---|---|---|---|
| Washing machine 640 × 580 | Washing machine 640 × 580 | Washing machine 640 × 580 | |

$(2 \times 560) + (2 \times 580) = 2280 < 2400$

So this arrangement fits in length-wise.

$600 + 640 = 1240 < 1250\,\text{mm}$

It also fits in breadth-wise so the delivery can be achieved in one trip.

# Section 2.5 Using precedence tables

## What you should know

- ★ How to list a set of tasks to complete a 'job'.
- ★ You will need to be able to put them in the order they need to be done — and decide if more than one task could be done at the same time.
- ★ You will need to know how long each task takes.
- ★ This information will be put into a precedence table, from which you will draw a 'network diagram' or a 'critical path analysis', which will tell you the total amount of time required to complete the job.

## Key words

task, job, activity
precedence table
network diagram, activity network
critical path analysis

## Example 1

The Walter Bicycle Company is setting up its production line, ready for the Christmas rush.

The diagram shows the main parts of a bicycle that needs to be assembled.

The production manager draws up the following precedence table, which shows how each bicycle is put together by different people, carrying out different tasks.

| Task | Description | Time (minutes) | Preceded by |
|------|-------------|----------------|-------------|
| A | Prepare frame | 10 | – |
| B | Mount and align front wheel | 6 | A |
| C | Mount and align rear wheel | 6 | A |
| D | Attach crank and chain wheel | 3 | A |
| E | Attach chain wheel/crank to frame | 3 | D |
| F | Mount left pedal | 5 | D, E |
| G | Mount right pedal | 5 | D, E |
| H | Fix saddle, chain, stickers | 8 | A, B, C, D, E, F, G |

Using this precedence table, construct an activity network and determine how long it would take to put together one bicycle.

## Solution

Draw a table with the tasks in two columns, and join up letters that are preceded by another task:

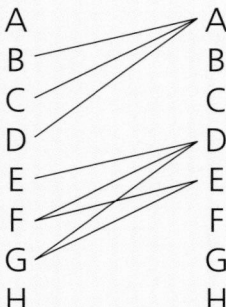                    (H would be linked to all)

List tasks in first column not linked to second column:

   A

   So A is the first task.

Delete A and all links from it, and re-write the table:

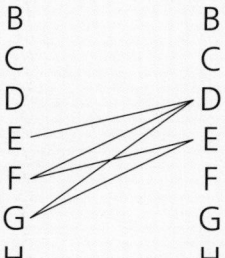

B          B
C          C
D          D
E          E
F          F
G          G
H          H          (H would be linked to all)

List tasks in first column not linked to second column:

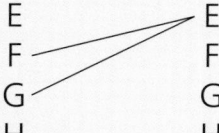

B   C   D ——————— These can be done at the same time.

Redraw (deleting all links to B, C, D):

E          E
F          F
G          G
H          H          (H would be linked to all)

List tasks in first column not linked to second column:

E

So E would be next.

Repeat the process to get F and G, and then finally H.

Now the activity network can be drawn up:

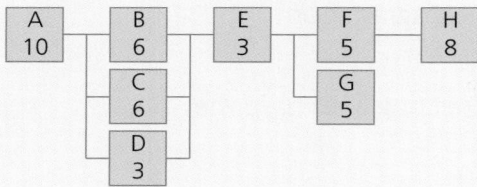

So the time required to put together one bicycle is (taking the longest task from each section):

$10 + 6 + 3 + 5 + 8 = 32$ minutes

## Example 2

Tommy, Nita and their two children are planning a day out for a picnic. There are some jobs they have to do to prepare for the trip.

All the family can help with the jobs, some of which must be done before others, while some can be done at the same time.

The table shows the tasks to be done, and the time each will take.

| Task | Description | Time (minutes) | Preceded by |
|------|-------------|----------------|-------------|
| A | Wash car | 30 | – |
| B | Wipe car dry | 15 | A |
| C | Wax and polish car | 30 | B |
| D | Prepare picnic | 40 | – |
| E | Clear kitchen | 5 | D |
| F | Pack picnic basket | 15 | D |

**a)** Construct an activity network.

**b)** By following the critical path, determine the latest time the family can begin to prepare if they wish to leave by 09·30.

## Solution

**a)** It can be seen that there are two distinct sets of tasks; those connected with the car and those connected with the picnic. This implies that it will be possible to do some tasks at the same time.

This example uses a different style of network diagram from Example 1 — either method is acceptable.

In this one the tasks are set out, and the connecting lines have the time for each task written along them.

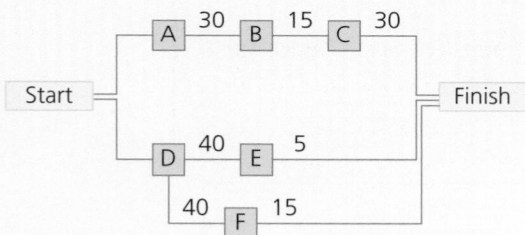

**b)** The paths can now be 'traced' to check on the time taken along each path. Three paths can be taken:

Start  A → B → C → Finish          30 + 15 + 30 = 75 minutes

Start  D → E → Finish                    40 + 5 = 45 minutes

Start  D → F → Finish                    40 + 15 = 55 minutes

So the critical path is A → B → C, which indicates that 75 minutes is the least amount of time required to complete all the tasks. Therefore if the family wish to leave at 09·30, they must start preparing no later than 08·15.

# Section 2.6 Use time management

## What you should know

★ As well as 'normal' speed/distance/time questions, this topic will also include travelling across time zones and the effects this may have on, for example, what time of day you could call a friend.

★ You may also be asked to use time management skills to plan, for example, programming of television shows or recording onto a disk.

★ You may be asked to take account of time zones to decide when it would be appropriate to have a 'conference call'.

## Key words

time, time management, time zones, time differences
speed, distance, time
order activities, start, finish

## Example 1

Consider a return flight from London to Tokyo. The average journey times are:

● London–Tokyo: 11 hours 30 minutes
● Tokyo–London: 12 hours 20 minutes

The time difference is due to prevailing winds around the globe.

**a)** A flight leaves Tokyo at 1230 hours *local time*. At what time will it arrive in London, *local time*, given that Tokyo time is *9 hours ahead* of London time?

**b)** Copy and complete this table, filling in the missing times (all times local):

| Tokyo | Departs | 0730 | 1000 | 1230 | 1730 | 2230 |
|---|---|---|---|---|---|---|
| London | Arrives | ? | ? | ? | ? | ? |

**c)** Suppose the airline has decided to run *three* daily flights from Tokyo to London. Design a possible schedule that will give convenient departure times for passengers.

**d)** Each plane must spend at least 3 hours at each airport, for disembarking, cleaning, refuelling, movement of luggage etc. Design a possible complete schedule for Tokyo–London–Tokyo for *three* daily services each day of the week, in each direction. How many planes are needed to cover this schedule? ⇨

⇨
# Solution

**a)** Note that going from Tokyo to London, the travel time is 12 hours 20 minutes *but* Tokyo is 9 hours ahead of London (so travel time could be considered as 3 hours 20 minutes).

So a flight leaving Tokyo at 1230 will arrive in London (local time) at 1230 + 3 hours 20 min = 1550.

**b)** The table could be completed by adding 3 hours 20 minutes to each flight departure time:

0730 → 1050, 1000 → 1320 and so on.

**c)** At this stage there is no indication of restrictions to planes, so suitable times could be, for example, early morning, middle of the day and early evening. Perhaps 0730, 1230 and 1530 — but at this stage, with no further information, times are open. The next part of the question asks you to take this to the next stage.

**d)** It is only when the conditions for this part (3 hours at the airport and three flights) come into play that you need to show some reasoning and justification for your suggestions.

Take an early time, say 0700, as an example:
- Leave Tokyo at 0700.
- Arrive London 1020.
- Wait 3 hours (1320).
- Fly back to Tokyo (flight time 11 hours 30 min) = 2450 + 9 hours ahead = 3350. This is 0950 the following day.
- Allow 3 hours wait time = 1250. This could be second departure (arrive in London 1610).

This would give something like:

Plane 1

Tokyo 0700 → London 1020 → Wait 3 hours → Tokyo 0950 (next day)

Plane 2

Tokyo 1250 → London 1610 → Wait 3 hours → Tokyo 1540 (next day)

(allows 3 hours at Tokyo before departure)

Plane 3

Tokyo 1840 → London 2200 → Tokyo 2130 (next day)

(allows 3 hours at Tokyo before departure)

So the three planes 'recycle'.

This would give reasonable times for departure from Tokyo, as well as good landing times (and departure) times from London.

If three planes left at the departure times on, say, Monday then two would be OK for Tuesday (the 1250 and 1840 flights), so a fourth plane would be needed to cover the Tuesday 0700 flight. ⇨

The 1840 flight (plane 3) on Monday would not arrive back until 2130.

Adding on the 3 hour turnaround, this would be 0030 on the Wednesday morning.

The company could use the time between 0030 and 0700 to carry out further safety checks, deep cleaning and so on.

This would allow the plane to be used for the 0700 flight.

The cycle then continues with each plane, in turn, having this time for safety checks and cleaning.

A timetable could look something like this:

| Departure time | Monday | Tuesday | Wednesday | Thursday | Friday |
|---|---|---|---|---|---|
| 0700 | Plane 1 | Plane 4 | Plane 3 | Plane 2 | Plane 1 |
| 1250 | Plane 2 | Plane 1 | Plane 4 | Plane 3 | Plane 2 |
| 1840 | Plane 3 | Plane 2 | Plane 1 | Plane 4 | Plane 3 |

## Example 2

Mike is working in Beijing, China, which is 8 hours ahead of UK time.

Pat is in Edinburgh, and Alan is in Bremen, Germany, which is 1 hour ahead of UK time.

All three work between 9 am and 6 pm local time.

Mike wants to make a conference call, lasting 1 hour, when all three are at work.

When would be a suitable (Beijing) time to call, and what would be the local times in Edinburgh and Bremen?

## Solution

Consider the working days:

- Beijing            9 am → 6 pm
- Edinburgh (−8) 1 am → 10 am
- Bremen (UK + 1) 2 am → 11 am

So Mike should call at 5 pm until 6 pm. This allows the last hour of work.

In Edinburgh this would be 9 am–10 am — Pat's first hour at work and in Bremen it would be 10 am–11 am.

# Section 2.7 Consider the effects of tolerance

## What you should know

* ★ How to work out upper and lower limits, given a tolerance.
  For example, 3 cm ± 2 mm (lower limit 3 cm − 0·2 cm = 2·8 cm,
  upper limit 3 cm + 0·2 cm = 3·2 cm).
* ★ How to compare, for example, samples of items to check how
  many fall within acceptable limits, and make recommendations
  based on this.
* ★ You will need to be able to state the effects tolerance/error has on
  measurements such as area and volume.
* ★ You will need to consider tolerance in terms of compatibility of fitting.

## Key words

tolerance, error
upper/lower limit
upper/lower bounds
interval, acceptable, nominal

## Example 1

Euan is in training for a 400 metre race. He states that he can
run 400 metres in 44 seconds.

You would expect this in paper 2.

Both of these measurements are given to
2 significant figures.

Find his maximum speed.

### Solution

400 m to 2 significant figures could be from
395 m (lowest) to 405 m (highest), that is 400 ± 5 m.

Distance: 400 ± 5 m  low = 395 m  high = 405 m

Similarly, speed: 44 ± 0·5 s          low = 43·5 s          high = 44·5 s

$$\text{maximum speed} = \frac{\text{greatest distance}}{\text{shortest time}}$$

$$= \frac{405}{43·5}$$

$$= 9·31 \text{ metres per second}$$

$$= 9·3 \text{ to 2 significant figures}$$

Note that this involves numeracy (significant figures).

## Example 2

A sack of sand weighs 20 kg ± 0·5 kg. It is used to fill bags that will contain 250 g of sand measured to the nearest 10 g.

Work out the maximum number of bags that can be filled.

### Solution

To find the maximum number of bags that can be filled, we need the maximum possible weight of the sack and the minimum possible weight in each bag.

Then we need to divide the maximum sack weight by the minimum bag weight.

The *maximum* weight for the sack is 20·5 kg (20 ± 0·5 kg).

The *minimum* weight for each bag is 245 g (250 ± 5 g).

Before we can divide, the units need to be the same.

Convert kilograms into grams by multiplying by 1000:

20·5 kg = 20 500 g

$$\frac{20\ 500}{245} = 83·67\ldots$$  ⟶ Note that this uses numeracy: converting units and appropriate rounding.

Normally we would round 83·67… to 84 but in this case it is not practical because the last bag did not fill completely. Therefore the maximum number of bags that could be filled is 83.

## Example 3

Tom makes bolts and screws. One type of bolt he makes is 5·1 ± 0·05 cm long and has a diameter of 1·5 ± 0·05 cm

Jerry sells drill bits. All the drill bits Jerry sells have a tolerance of ± 0·025 cm

If Tom buys a drill bit of nominal size 1·5 cm from Jerry, what problems may he encounter?

### Solution

Key word: *tolerance*

Consider diameter of bolt:

1·5 ± 0·05        lower limit = 1·45 cm        upper limit = 1·55 cm

Consider diameter of drill bit:

1·5 ± 0·025        lower limit = 1·475 cm        upper limit = 1·525 cm

So at the upper limit, the bolt could be too big for the hole drilled by the drill bit.

# Section 2.8 Investigate situations involving gradient

## What you should know

★ How to calculate the gradient of a slope and perhaps compare this with a condition — for example, checking if a slope is less than 1 in 12.

## Key words

gradient, slope
vertical, horizontal
run, rise
height, distance

## Example 1

Building guidelines for accessibility state that:

● the maximum gradient of a ramp shall be 1 in 12

● the maximum rise shall be 760 mm for any length of run.

(Rise is the vertical distance of a ramp and run is the horizontal distance.)

rise |
run

Does this ramp meet the two guidelines?

0·6 m |
7·8 m

## Solution

Key word: *gradient* (gradient $= \dfrac{\text{vertical}}{\text{horizontal}}$ )

gradient $= \dfrac{0·6}{7·8}$ ———— Multiply the top and bottom by 10.

$= \dfrac{6}{78}$

$= \dfrac{1}{13}$ ———— Compare the answer with $\dfrac{1}{12}$.

So the gradient is $\dfrac{1}{13}$, which is less than $\dfrac{1}{12}$, so it meets guideline 1.

0·6 m = 600 mm ———— Convert 0·6 m to mm.

This is less than 760 mm, so it meets guideline 2.

## Example 2

The formula for relating the depth of treads and the height of risers on a set of stairs was developed by François Blondel, a French architect, in the seventeenth century.

Based on observations of how people walked up and down stairs, the formula suggested that twice the riser height plus the tread depth should be between 610 mm and 635 mm.

In other words, the 'steepness' of the stairs should fit into this formula:

$610 < (2 \times \text{riser}) + \text{tread} < 635$

Would this set of stairs fit with Blondel's formula?

160mm
←310mm→

riser
tread

### Solution

Use the formula:

$(2 \times \text{riser}) + \text{tread} = (2 \times 160) + 310$

$= 630 \, \text{mm}$

So, yes, the stairs do fit in with the formula because $610 < 630 < 635$.

# Section 2.9 Area of composite shapes

## What you should know

★ How to calculate the area of basic shapes and composite shapes — for example, a rectangle compounded with a triangle, or a square with a semi-circle.
★ You could be asked to work out the area of a sector of a circle.
★ Typical questions could include areas of gardens with irregular shapes, or windows, or areas of sections of an athletics field.

## Key words

shape, composite, area
circle, sector

# Example 1

This road sign is in the shape of a rectangle with a triangular end.

Calculate the area of metal required to make this sign

75 cm

20 cm

40 cm

DETOUR

## Solution

Key words: *shape, area*

Split the shape into basic parts — in this case a rectangle and a triangle.

area = length × breadth $\qquad$ area = $\frac{1}{2}$ × base × height —— Write down the formulae.

$\qquad$ = 75 cm × 40 cm $\qquad\qquad$ = $\frac{1}{2}$ × 40 cm × 20 cm —— Substitute

$\qquad$ = 3000 cm$^2$ $\qquad\qquad\qquad$ = 400 cm$^2$ —— Calculate

total area of metal = 3400 cm$^2$ —— State the answer (with units).

# Example 2

A swimming pool in a holiday resort is in the shape of a rectangle with a semi-circular end.

Calculate its area. ——  The numbers have been chosen so that this could be a paper 1 question.

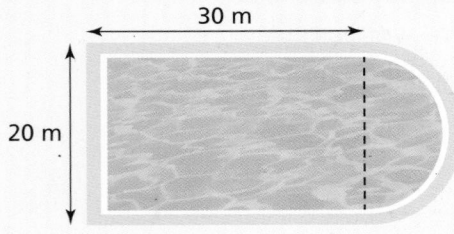

30 m

20 m

⇨

## Solution

Split into two shapes — a rectangle and a semi-circle:

area = length × breadth          area = $\frac{1}{2} \times \pi \times r^2$ ————— Write down the formulae.

     = 30 × 20 .               = $\frac{1}{2} \times 3\cdot14 \times 10^2$ ————— Substitute

     = 600 m$^2$             = $\frac{1}{2} \times 314 = 157$ m$^2$ ————— Calculate

total area = 757 m$^2$ ————— State the answer (with units).

This topic is an ideal one for including in a case study in paper 2 — for example, area and perimeter of a field and the cost of fencing and turfing.

## Example 3

Jennifer has an ornamental garden as shown in the diagram.
She wants to put a 'log roll' edging around it.
Log roll comes in 2-metre sections costing £8·15 per section.
Jennifer also wishes to seed it as lawn.
Packets of grass seed, each of which will cover 5 m$^2$, cost £6·49.
How much will it cost Jennifer to edge and seed the lawn?

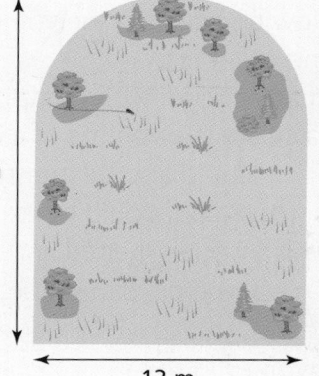

16 m

12 m

### Solution

Calculate the perimeter:

perimeter = (3 × straight edges) + semi-circle

      = 12 + 10 + 10 + ½π$d$ ————— $d$ = 12 and 10 is the length of the side up to the curved area

      = 32 + 18·84

      = 50·84 m

      = 52 m required (comes in 2 m sections)

      = 26 sections ————— State the answer with a reason.

26 sections @ £8·15 = £211·90

⇨

Calculate the area:

area = rectangle + semi-circle

$$= lb + \tfrac{1}{2}\pi r^2$$

$$= (12 \times 10) + \tfrac{1}{2}\pi 6^2$$

$$= 176\cdot52\,\text{m}^2$$

grass seed = 176·52/5

$$= 35\cdot3 \quad\text{————— Need to round up in this case.}$$

36 packets of grass seed @ £6·49 = £233·64

total cost = £211·90 + £233·64

$$= £445\cdot54$$

# Section 2.10 Volume of composite solids

## What you should know

- ★ How to calculate the volume of basic solids such as cubes, cuboids and cylinders.
- ★ In association with composite solids, you should be able to calculate the volume of a cone or a sphere (formulae will be given).
- ★ There could also be questions on the 'conservation of volume'. This is where you would be expected to calculate the volume of a solid, which is then melted and formed into another shape. For example, a medicine pill is in shape of a sphere. The company decides to change this to a cylinder, and you will have to do calculations involved in this.

## Key words

volume, basic prisms (cube, cuboid, cylinder)
composite solids
conservation
other solids (cone, sphere, hemisphere)

## Example 1

This packing box has dimensions length 60 cm, width 40 cm and height 20 cm.

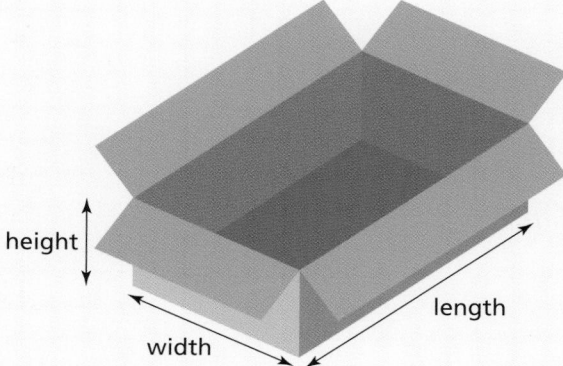

This cylinder with area of base 400 cm² has half the volume of the box.

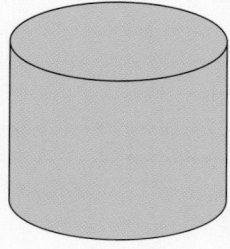

**a)** What is the volume of the packing box?

**b)** Will the cylinder fit on a shelf that has height of 65 cm?

## Solution

**a)** volume = length × width × height ─── Write down the formula.

$\quad\quad$ = 60 × 40 × 20 ─── Substitute

$\quad\quad$ = 48 000 cm³ ─── Calculate and state the answer (with units).

**b)** volume of cylinder = area of base × height

$\quad$ ½ × volume of box = 24 000

$\quad\quad\quad\quad\quad\quad$ = 400 × height

$\quad\quad$ 60 cm = height

So, yes, the cylinder will fit since 60 < 65. ─── State the answer with a reason.

## Example 2

A plastic paper clip holder is made out of a cuboid with a  hemisphere cut out of it.

The dimensions are as follows:

- length 12 cm
- breadth 12 cm
- height 5 cm
- diameter of hemisphere 8 cm

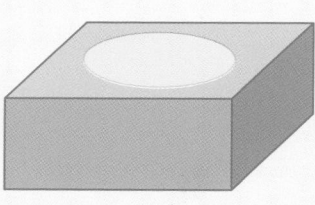

$\Rightarrow$

**a)** Calculate the volume of plastic used.

**b)** If 1 cm³ of plastic weighs 1·52 g, what is the weight of the paper-clip holder?

## Solution

**a)** volume = cuboid − hemisphere

$$= lbh - (½ \times \frac{4}{3} \times \pi r^3)$$

The volume of a sphere will be given in the formula list.

$$= (12 \times 12 \times 5) - (½ \times \frac{4}{3} \times \pi \times 4^3)$$

$$= 586 \text{ cm}^3 \text{ to the nearest cm}^3$$

**b)** weight = 586 × 1·52 g

$$= 890·72 \text{ g}$$

# Section 2.11 Use Pythagoras' theorem in a two-stage calculation

## What you should know 👍

★ How to calculate the hypotenuse, or one of the shorter sides, in a right-angled triangle. Typically you will need to do this twice to solve a given problem.
★ Another context may be to apply Pythagoras to circle problems — such as depth of oil in a pipe, depth of milk in a tanker or width of surface water in a drain.

## Key words

Pythagoras, hypotenuse
converse
two-stage, 3D
space diagonal

## Example 1

A packing case has dimensions length 50 cm × breadth 50 cm × height 60 cm.

Will a curtain pole of length 1 m fit in the 'space diagonal'?

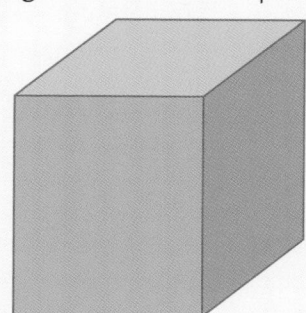

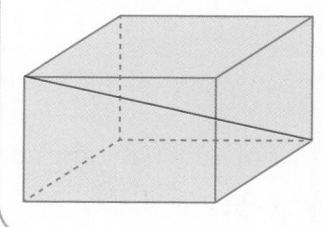

## Solution

Work out the diagonal of the base (using Pythagoras' theorem):

diagonal$^2$ = 50$^2$ + 50$^2$ ——————— Substitute

= 5000 ——————— Calculate

diagonal = 70·7 cm

space diagonal$^2$ = 70·7$^2$ + 60$^2$ ——————— Stage 2

= 8598·5

space diagonal = 92·7 cm

So the curtain pole will *not* fit since 1 m > 92·7 cm. ——— State the answer (with a reason).

## Example 2

The jib of a crane is as shown in the diagram (AD).
Calculate the length of the 'raising rod' marked AB.

## Solution

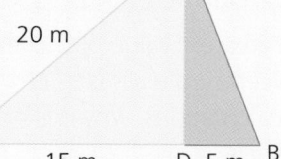

First, calculate the height from A to D:

(AD)$^2$ = 20$^2$ − 15$^2$

= 175 ——————— No need to take the square root as we will use this value later.

Use this in the second step:

(AB)$^2$ = (AD)$^2$ + 5$^2$

= 175 + 25

= 200

AB = $\sqrt{200}$

= 14·1 m to 1 decimal place

## Example 3

The diagram shows a tanker partly full with milk.

The surface of the milk is 3 m across.

The radius of the tank is 2 m.

Calculate the depth of the milk.

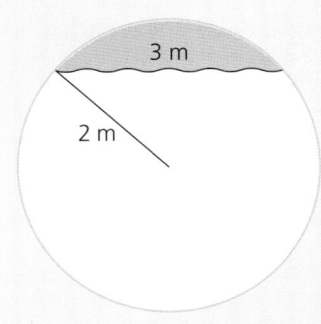

## Solution

Identify the right-angled triangle (see dotted lines):

By Pythagoras:

$x^2 = 2^2 - 1.5^2$

$= 1.75$

$x = 1.3$ m to 1 decimal place

depth of milk $= 1.3 + 2$ (radius)

$= 3.3$ m

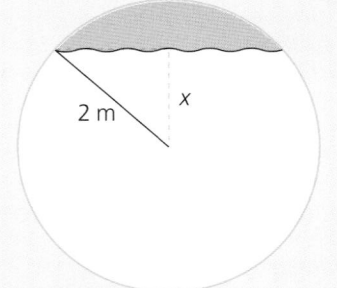

## Practice questions

1  Plastic bricks are made in the form of cubes. The length of each brick is 11·3 cm, measured correct to the nearest mm.

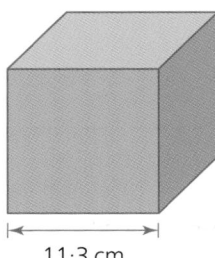

11·3 cm

a)  Write down the least and greatest value of the length of a brick.

b)  The length of a shelf between two walls is 91 cm ± 0·5 cm.
   Explain, showing all your calculations, why it is not always possible to place eight bricks on the shelf.

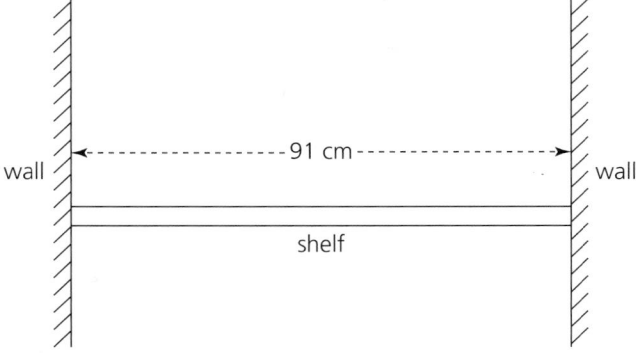

2  Which of these shapes has the larger capacity? Show your working.

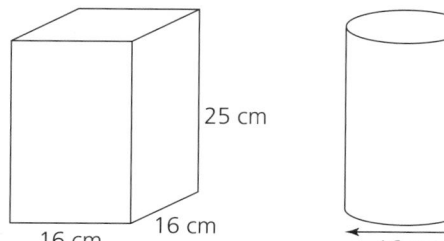

25 cm

25 cm

16 cm   16 cm

16 cm

3  The dimensions of a standard '8 ft' container are shown below:

- ○ Outside length 2·44 m (8ft)
- ○ Outside height 2·26 m
- ○ Outside width 2·2 m
- ○ Internal length 2·29 m
- ○ Internal height 2·06 m
- ○ Internal width 2·11 m
- ○ Door width 2·1 m
- ○ Door height 1·95 m

a) Write down, in metres, the internal length, width and height.

b) What is the volume, in cubic metres, of this container?

c) What is the length of the space diagonal?

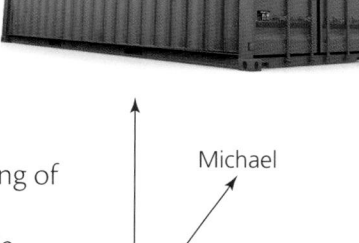

4  Amanda and Michael leave the same campsite and set off in different directions. Michael walks 7 km on a bearing of 035° and Amanda walks 8 km due east.

a) Using a scale of 1 cm:1 km make a scale drawing of their journey.

b) Use your drawing to find how far apart Amanda and Michael are.

c) On what bearing should Amanda walk to get to Michael's position?

Michael

35°

Amanda

5  A ramp is being designed to allow wheelchair access to a vet's surgery. Regulations state that the slope must not be greater than 1 in 15. The ramp has to achieve a height of 30 cm.
What is the minimum distance from the building the ramp would have to start in order to meet these regulations?

6  Temperature is often measured in degrees Celsius, °C, or degrees Fahrenheit, °F.

The freezing point of water is 0°C and 32°F. The boiling point of water is 100°C and 212°F.
Is there a temperature at which Celsius and Fahrenheit readings are the same?
Hint: drawing a graph might help.

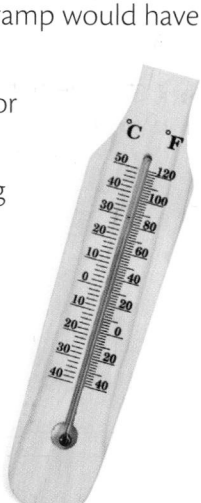

7   A baby's teething toy is made from adding two identical cones to a cylinder as shown.

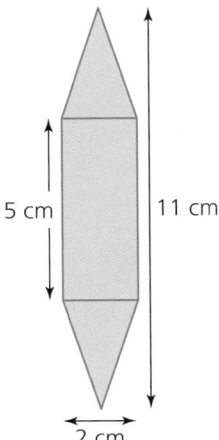

5 cm    11 cm

2 cm

Calculate the volume of the teething toy. The formula for the volume of a cone is $\frac{1}{3}\pi r^2 h$.

8   Carol makes toy plastic bricks for children's playrooms.
The length of a brick is 22·0 cm, the width 10·0 cm and the height 8·0 cm.
All measurements are to the nearest 0·05 cm.

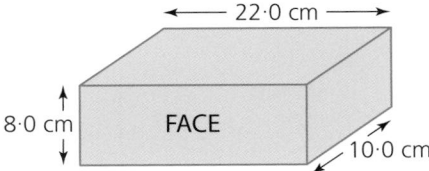

22·0 cm

8·0 cm    FACE

10·0 cm

   a) Write down the upper and lower limits of the dimensions of the brick.
   b) Write down the upper and lower limits of the area of the face of the brick marked 'face'.
   c) Write down the upper and lower limits of the volume of the brick.
   d) Compare your answers for the area of the face in b) and the volume in c) to those of the 'nominal' values.

9   Jessica is designing a sports bag for her sports club, as shown.

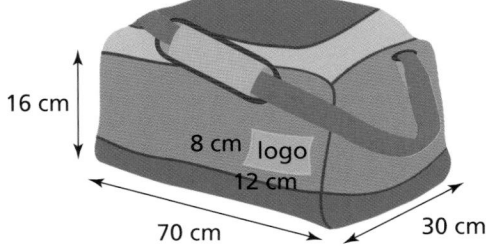

16 cm

8 cm  logo
12 cm

70 cm         30 cm

Her sports federation states that a logo cannot take up more than 10% of the area of the face on which it is placed.
Does Jessica's design meet the requirements of her sports federation?

10 The diagram shows a restaurant door.

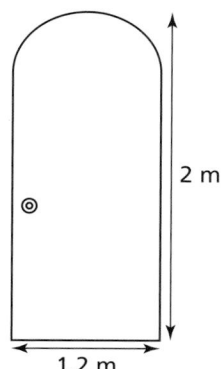

2 m

1.2 m

Calculate the area of the door.

11 Megan has two pieces of wood, which she places end to end.
One piece has length 5·3 ± 0·05 cm, the other 7·4 ± 0·02 cm
Find the minimum and maximum total lengths.

12 Three radio stations, Alpha, Beta and Gamma, are positioned as shown.

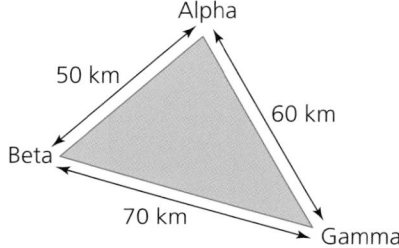

Alpha

50 km

60 km

Beta

70 km

Gamma

Broadcasts from Alpha can be heard within a radius of 30 km.
From Beta, broadcasts can be heard at distance of up to 40 km, and from
Gamma they can be heard within a distance of 45 km.
a) Draw an accurate scale drawing to show the boundaries of the three
broadcast receiving areas.
b) Shade in the region where all three broadcasts can be heard.

# Chapter 3
# Numeracy and data

## Unit requirements

This unit has two stated outcomes:

* Use numerical skills to solve real-life problems involving money/time/measurement.
* Interpret graphical data and situations involving probability to solve real-life problems involving money/time/measurement.

Numerical skills include:

* selecting and using appropriate numerical notation and units
* selecting and carrying out calculations
* recording measurements (length, angle, weight, volume and temperature) using a scale on an instrument
* interpreting measurements and the results of calculations to make decisions
* justifying decisions by using the results of measurements and calculations

Data skills include:

* extracting and interpreting data from at least three different graphical forms
* making and justifying decisions using evidence from the interpretation of data
* making and justifying decisions based on probability

# What kinds of question might you be asked?

## Numeracy section

● You may be asked to work using appropriate units.
● You may be asked to carry out calculations involving, for example, addition, subtraction, multiplication and division with fractions and decimals. Rounding, significant figures and mixed numbers will also feature.
● You may be asked to carry out calculations involving percentages; including percentage increase, decrease, a percentage of, one quantity as a percentage of another, compound percentages such as interest, appreciation and depreciation.
● You may be asked to carry out speed, distance and time calculations.

- There could be questions on area and volume (including surface area).
- You may be asked questions involving ratio, scale, direct proportion and inverse proportion.
- You could be asked to read and interpret measurements using, for example, a ruler, a protractor or temperature gauges.
- You will be asked to use your readings and calculations to justify a decision or to make a recommendation.

# Data section

- You may be asked to interpret a table, or extract information where the table contains a number of rows and columns covering a number of 'categories'.
- You may need to draw or complete charts or graphs where parts are missing, where parts are not obvious or there are misleading parts on the graph/chart.
- You need to be familiar with different types of graphs and charts such as stem-and-leaf, scatter diagrams or maps.
- You will need to be able to look for trends or relationships upon which to base a recommendation, or make a justification.
- You may need to show that you understand how bias and sample size can affect your choices, decisions and recommendations.
- You may need to use patterns and trends to help you state the probability of an event happening.
- You will need to be able to calculate the probability of an event happening.
- You may also be asked to calculate the probability of combined events, and to consider effects of bias.
- Probability may be described through use of percentages, decimals, fractions and ratios.

Later in this section we will look at some questions and how they should be answered. Remember that short questions will only ask about one topic but longer questions can involve two or three topics — and not all from the same section:

- The numeracy section, in particular, will use contexts from other units — for example, using your numeracy skills to work with money, or with speed–distance–time questions.
- You may use measurement readings in connection with tolerance.
- Ratio and scale are obvious partners to bearings and navigation.
- In the data section you may find there is an overlap with the statistics section in the 'Managing finance and statistics' unit.
- Another example would be in using probability with tolerance, or with risk of borrowing money.

Remember that the questions in paper 1 are non-calculator, so you need to be able to work comfortably with all the numerical skills outlined above. Questions in this paper will vary from short (2–3 marks), to medium (3–5 marks) to extended (4–6 marks). Longer questions will probably be broken down into parts a, b and possibly c.

Paper 2 will involve case studies varying from short (around 4 marks) to extended (up to around 15 marks). Remember that longer questions could involve topics from the other units — that is, there may be some finance and statistics or some geometry and measures topics in the question.

Let us look at some typical questions for this unit.

# Section 3.1 Select and use appropriate numerical notation and units

## What you should know

★ How to select and use appropriate units for money, time and measurement.
★ Measurement could include length, angle, weight, area, volume and temperature.
★ How to substitute into a simple formula and use 'BODMAS' to calculate values.

## Key words

millimetres, centimetres, kilometres
square units for area, cubic units for volume
degrees,
grams, kilograms,
litres, millilitres
seconds, minutes, hours, days, months, years
pounds, pence, other currencies (euro, kroner etc.)

## Hints & tips

Remember BODMAS (some people say BOMDAS or BIDMAS — the 'I' meaning 'index'):

✓ B = Brackets — do what is in (...) first
✓ O = Of — to the power of, or ¾ of, or 25% of
✓ DM = Divide/Multiply — do this in the order they appear, left to right
✓ AS = Add/Subtract — do these last to 'tidy up'

The following examples involve calculations — but it is important that you recognise the units that you should use and state.

## Example 1

At an athletics meet, Usain Bolt ran the 100 metres in a time of 9·785 seconds.

Round his time to:

**a)** two decimal places
**b)** two significant figures

### Solution

Key word: *round*

**a)** 9·7̲8̲5̲ ————

> Mark under the first two decimal places.
> Put a squiggle under the next one.
> Five or more you round up.

So 9·785 = 9·79 to two decimal places.

**b)** 9̲·7̲8̲5 ————————

> Mark under first two non-zero digits.
> Put a squiggle under the next one.
> Five or more you round up.

So 9·785 = 9·8 to two significant figures.

## Example 2

Jim Hines set a world record for the 100 metres sprint at the Mexico Olympics in 1968.

He won the race in 9·9 seconds.

There was a tailwind, which may have reduced his time by $\frac{3}{25}$ of a second. Estimate his time if there had been no tailwind.

### Solution

Add $\frac{3}{25}$ of a second to his time.

expected time = 9·9 + 0·12

$\qquad\qquad$ = 10·02 seconds

## Example 3

When buying kitchen units, the dimensions are normally given using millimetres (mm). For example, a 3-metre worktop would be described as 3000 mm.

**a)** A double base unit is 1·2 m wide. How would this be described?
**b)** A run of units consists of cupboards of 1 × 500 mm, 2 × 600 mm and 1 × 1200 mm. Would these units fit under a 3 m worktop?

### Solution

**a)** 1·2 m = 1200 mm wide
**b)** (1 × 500) + (2 × 600) + (1 × 1200) = 500 + 1200 + 1200

$\qquad\qquad\qquad\qquad\qquad\qquad$ = 2900 mm, which is less than
$\qquad\qquad\qquad\qquad\qquad\qquad\qquad$ 3000 mm (3 m)

Yes, the units would fit under a 3 m worktop.

# Section 3.2 Carrying out calculations

## What you should know

★ This section covers a number of arithmetical operations. Some of these operations will be used elsewhere in the course so you should be comfortable in their application.

★ You will be expected to be able to add, subtract, multiply and divide using a range of numbers.

★ You must be able to work to two decimal places (in money questions) — for example, multiplying money by a single digit or by 10, 100, 1000 (e.g. £5·20 per hour for 6 hours).

★ Numbers and answers should be rounded appropriately, using significant figures or decimal places. You need to be able to work to three decimal places (in number work other than money).

★ You will need to work with percentages and fractions, including compound percentage increase or decrease, percentage of a quantity, a quantity as a percentage of another, and converting between fractions, decimals and percentages.

★ You should be able to work with mixed numbers, add and subtract simple fractions and find the number of fractional parts in a mixed number — for example, 3¼ = 13 quarters.

★ How to calculate:
  – speed, distance and time
  – perimeter
  – area (including triangles and composite shapes)
  – volume (including cylinders and triangular prisms)
  – perimeter (including that of a circle — the circumference)
  – ratio, for example as part of scale drawing, or sharing out in a given ratio (e.g. sharing a dinner bill in a ratio of 3:2)
  – direct and indirect proportion

## Key words

decimals, fractions, percentages, compound
rounding, decimal places, significant figures
increase, decrease, appreciation, depreciation
mixed numbers
speed, distance, time
perimeter, area, volume
proportion, ratio, share

## Example 1

A map has a scale of 1:25 000. On the map, the distance between the leisure centre and the primary
school is 3 cm.

What is the actual distance between them?

### Solution

Key words: *map, scale, actual distance*

This tells you that we are going from scale to real.

So we will multiply by the scale.

> Look at the scale used. Are you going from small to large or from large to small?

| Map (cm) | Actual (cm) |
|----------|-------------|
| 1 | 25 000 |
| 3 | 25 000 × 3 = 75 000 cm = 750 m |

## Example 2

Three teams appeared in a final of the 4 × 100 m relay at an athletics event.

The runners who run the second, third and fourth legs usually post
quicker times than the first leg because they begin to run before
receiving the baton, rather than start from the blocks.

The times for the three teams are shown in the table below.

| Team | 1st leg (secs) | 2nd leg (secs) | 3rd leg (secs) | 4th leg (secs) |
|------|----------------|----------------|----------------|----------------|
| Arrows | 9·82 | 9·31 | 8·96 | 9·22 |
| Darts | 10·03 | $9\frac{1}{10}$ | $8\frac{4}{5}$ | $9\frac{1}{4}$ |
| Flights | 9·86 | $8\frac{17}{20}$ | $9\frac{1}{2}$ | 9·39 |

**a)** Which was the fastest leg in the race?
**b)** Which was the slowest?
**c)** Which team won the race?

61

## Solution

Redo the table – changing all fractions to decimals – so comparisons can be made.

| Team | 1st leg (secs) | 2nd leg (secs) | 3rd leg (secs) | 4th leg (secs) |
|------|----------------|----------------|----------------|----------------|
| Arrows | 9·82 | 9·31 | 8·96 | 9·22 |
| Darts | 10·03 | $9\frac{1}{10} = 9·10$ | $8\frac{4}{5} = 8·80$ | $9\frac{1}{4} = 9·25$ |
| Flights | 9·86 | $8\frac{17}{20} = 8·85$ | $9\frac{1}{2} = 9·50$ | 9·39 |

So now it is easy to compare times.

**a)** The fastest leg was the Darts 3rd leg

**b)** The slowest leg was the Darts 1st leg

**c)** To find winner, add up the times:

Arrows: $9·82 + 9·31 + 8·96 + 9·22 = 37·31$ seconds

Darts: $10·03 + 9·10 + 8·80 + 9·25 = 37·18$ seconds

Flights: $9·86 + 8·85 + 9·50 + 9·39 = 37·60$ seconds

So the winners were the Darts.

## Example 3

In a typical meal for a person trying to keep fit:

- $\frac{1}{4}$ of it should be protein

- $\frac{3}{20}$ of it should be fat

- the rest should be carbohydrates (including fruit and vegetables).

If the meal contained 240 g of carbohydrates, how much protein would you expect to be in the meal?

## Solution

Carbohydrates account for:

$$1 - \frac{1}{4} - \frac{3}{20} = 1 - \frac{5}{20} - \frac{3}{20}$$

$$= \frac{12}{20} \text{ of the meal}$$

So protein, which accounts for $\frac{5}{20}$ of the meal, would be:

$$\frac{5}{12} \times 240\,g = 100\,g$$

You would expect 100 g of protein in the meal.

## Example 4

In order to carry out repairs, an electricity sub-station cuts its output from 120 000 volts to 23 000 volts.

Express this reduction as a percentage of its usual output.

### Solution

reduction = 120 000 − 23 000 = 97 000

Convert to a percentage:

$$\frac{97\,000}{120\,000} \times 100 = 80.83333$$

$$= 80.8\% \text{ to 1 decimal place}$$

## Example 5

An electrical appliance rated at 1 kW, if used for 1 hour, would be responsible for about ½ kg of $CO_2$ emissions.

A television uses about 0.1 kW of power.

If a television was left on from 9 in the morning until 11 pm, how much $CO_2$ would it be responsible for?

### Solution

number of hours = 14 hours

Calculation: = 14 × 0.1

$$= 1.4 \text{ kW used}$$

$$= 1.4 \times ½$$

$$= 0.7 \text{ kg of } CO_2$$

## Example 6

John works as a braille translator in the Royal Blind School. He gets paid £24 per hour.

One day he worked 6⅔ hours. What was his pay?

### Solution

Calculate:

pay = 24 × 6⅔

$$= (24 \times 6) + (24 \times ⅔)$$ ——— Sometimes it is easier to split mixed numbers up and work with the whole number part and then the fraction part.

$$= 144 + 16$$

$$= 160$$

John earns £160. ——— Use the unit in the answer — in this case, money, so a £ sign.

## Example 7

Sharon thinks that if she invests her money at 12·5% compound interest, she will double her money in 6 years.

Is Sharon correct?

### Solution

Consider £1 invested at 12·5% for 6 years.

Calculate:

value after 6 years $= 1 \times 1 \cdot 125^6$

$$= 2 \cdot 03$$

> Compound interest question:
> - Get the multiplier correct – 6 because 6 years.
> - This is an increase, so 1 + ...

So after 6 years Sharon would have £2·03, so she would have doubled her money.

## Example 8

A beach volleyball court has dimensions as shown:

a) What is the area of the court?

b) What is the perimeter?

c) Tape, 10 cm wide, is used to mark out the perimeter of the court. What area of tape would be used?

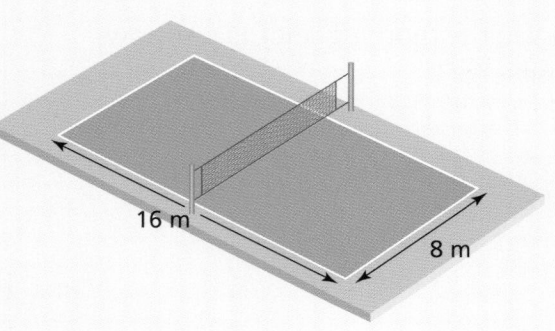

16 m

8 m

### Solution

a) area $=$ length $\times$ breadth

$$= 16 \times 8$$

$$= 128 \, m^2$$

b) perimeter $= (2 \times 16) + (2 \times 8)$

$$= 48 \, m$$

c) Area of tape:

width of tape $= 10 \, cm = 0 \cdot 1 \, m$

> When working with measures, make sure you are using same units.

area $= 0 \cdot 1 \times 48$

$$= 4 \cdot 8 \, m^2$$

## Example 9

A tin of kidney beans (cylinder) has a diameter of
7·6 cm and a height of 10 cm.

What is the volume?

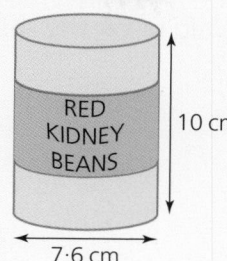

RED
KIDNEY
BEANS

10 cm

7·6 cm

### Solution

Key word: *volume*

volume = $\pi r^2 h$

$= 3{\cdot}14 \times 3{\cdot}8^2 \times 10$

$= 453{\cdot}4\,cm^3$

## Example 10

A box of Funny Cow cheese spread
is packaged as shown.

The dimensions are shown.

What is the volume of cheese spread
in the box, assuming the cheese spread
fills the packaging?

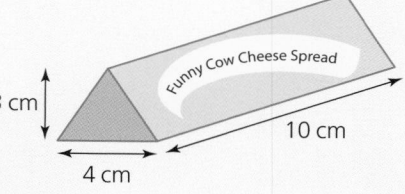

3 cm

Funny Cow Cheese Spread

10 cm

4 cm

### Solution

volume = area of base × length

$= \frac{1}{2} \times 4 \times 3 \times 10$

$= 60\,cm^3$

## Example 11

Sales of a DVD *The Escape from Eskbank* were 3015 in 2011.

In 2012 sales rose by 8%, but in 2013 they fell back by 4%.

How many were sold in 2013? ———————— Read the question carefully.

### Solution

Key words: *% rise, % fall*

increase in sales for 2012 = 8% of 3015

$= 241{\cdot}2$ ———— Round appropriately.

So sales in 2012 would be 3015 + 241 = 3256.

fall in sales for 2013 = 4% of 3256

$= 130{\cdot}24$

So sales would be 3256 − 130 = 3126.

## Example 12

A shelf is 32½ cm long.

**a)** How many books of width 2¾ cm would fit on the shelf?
**b)** What space would be left over?

## Solution

**a)** $32½ ÷ 2¾ = \dfrac{65}{2} ÷ \dfrac{11}{4}$

$= \dfrac{65}{2} × \dfrac{4}{11}$

$= \dfrac{130}{11}$

$= 11\dfrac{9}{11}$

So 11 books would fit on the shelf

**b)** 11 books would take up:

$11 × 2¾ \text{ cm} = 11 × \dfrac{11}{4}$

$= \dfrac{121}{4}$

$= 30¼ \text{ cm}$

left over space $= 32½ - 30¼$

$= 2¼ \text{ cm}$

## Example 13

Three friends, Jane, Mary and Bob, share the cost of a raffle ticket in the ratio 4:3:1.

If they won a prize of £2000, how much should each get if it was shared in the same ratio?

## Solution

Key words: *ratio*

The ratio is 4:3:1 so $4 + 3 + 1 = 8$ shares.

Jane should get $\dfrac{4}{8}$ of £2000 = £1000

Mary should get $\dfrac{3}{8}$ of £2000 = £750

Bob should get $\dfrac{1}{8}$ of £2000 = £250

## Example 14

Jennifer's pay is in direct proportion to the number of hours she works.

One week she works 35 hours and gets pay of £253·75.

What would she be paid in a week in which she works 27 hours?

### Solution

Key words: *direct proportion*

Set up a table:

| Hours | Pay (£) |
|---|---|
| 35 | 253·75 |
| 27 | Less (so smaller number goes on top) <br> $= 253\cdot75 \times \dfrac{27}{35}$ <br> $= 195\cdot75$ |

Jennifer would expect to get £195·75 for working 27 hours.

# Section 3.3 Recording measurements

## What you should know

★ How to use a scale on a measuring instrument to record to the nearest marked or minor unnumbered division for length, angle, weight, volume and temperature. This may be done as a practical exercise using a variety of measuring instruments.
★ Evidence of success could be part of drawing a navigation course — i.e. making good use of a ruler and protractor.
★ You may get an example of reading the weights of baggage on scales and determining if the total load is within acceptable limits.

## Key words

scale, measure, read
record, indicate, state
instrument

## Example 1

Here is a section of an orienteering course.

What is the bearing of checkpoint B from checkpoint A?

## ⇨ Solution

Key word: *bearing*

Use your protractor.

Mark in the north arrow.

Connect the checkpoints with a line.

Place your protractor carefully.

Read the nearest (probably unnumbered) mark on the scale.

The bearing is 172°.

In this case you were reading unnumbered marks between 170 and 175 (or perhaps 180) degrees (which are marked on the protractor).

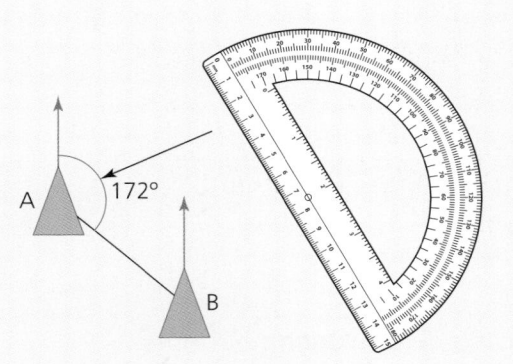

## Example 2 🚩

These scales show the weights of five furniture flat-packs.

A van has a load capacity of 350 kilograms.

Could all the flat-packs be put on this van?

Scale 1

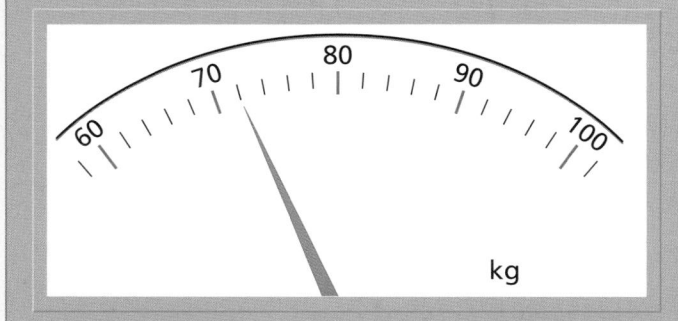

kg

Scale 2

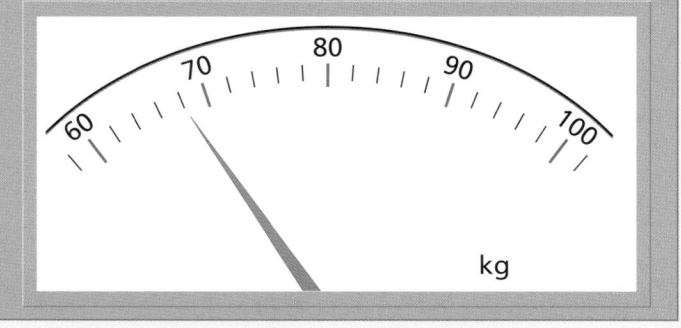

kg

⇨

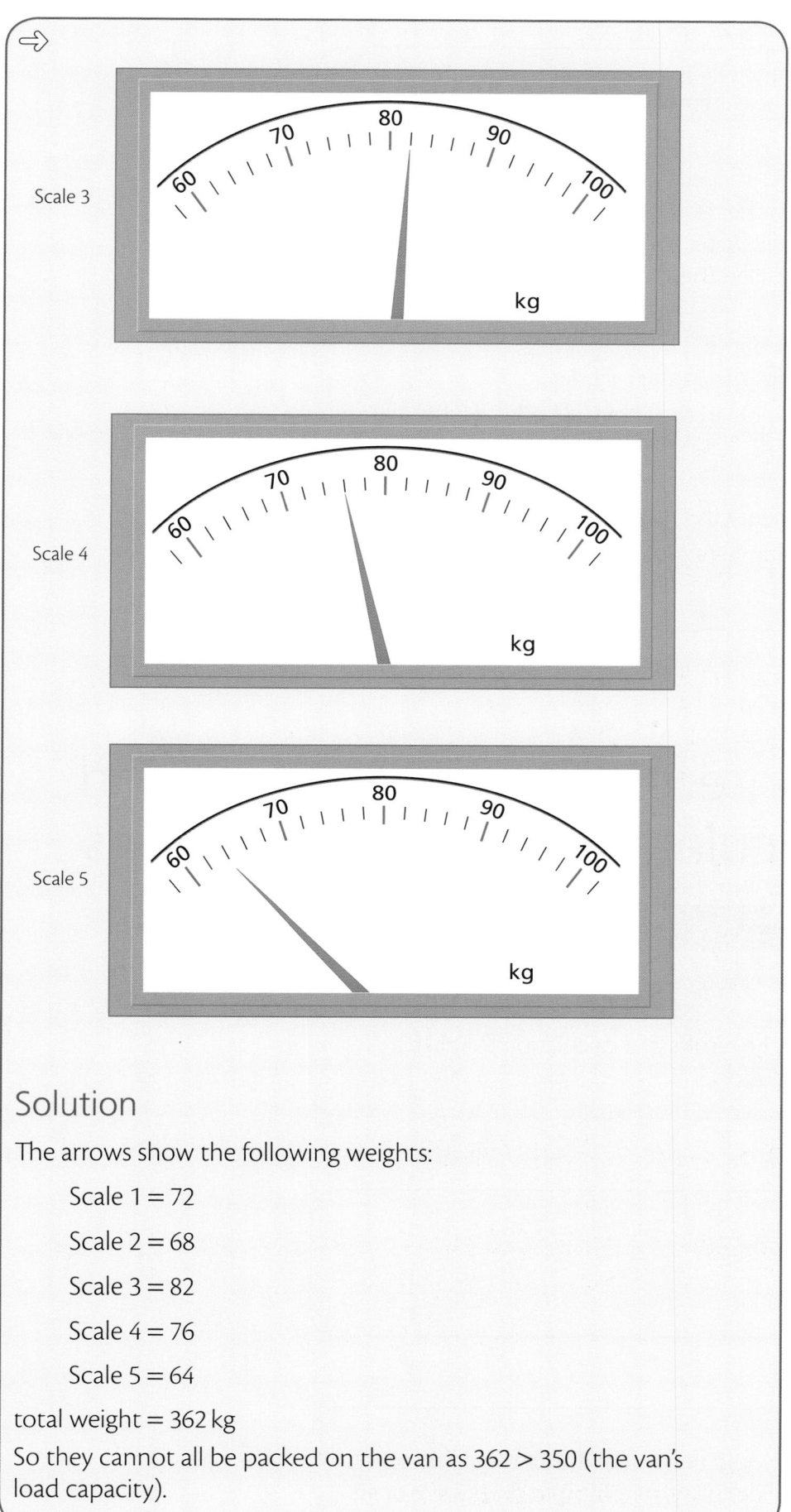

Scale 3

Scale 4

Scale 5

## Solution

The arrows show the following weights:

Scale 1 = 72

Scale 2 = 68

Scale 3 = 82

Scale 4 = 76

Scale 5 = 64

total weight = 362 kg

So they cannot all be packed on the van as 362 > 350 (the van's load capacity).

## Example 3

The diagram shows a liquid measurement taken in a cylindrical flask.

The liquid surface is curved (U-shaped) rather than horizontal, due to the relatively strong attractive force between water and glass. (This curved surface is called the meniscus.)

As a general rule, the bottom of the meniscus is taken as the liquid level in the cylinder.

What would be the level of liquid in the above cylindrical flask?

### Solution

Look at the bottom of the meniscus.

Identify how much each unnumbered mark is worth (in this case 1 ml).

So the level of liquid is 54 ml.

# Section 3.4 Interpret measurements and results of calculations to make decisions

## What you should know

★ How to identify relevant measurements and/or the significance of the result of a calculation.
★ You may be asked to use the results of a calculation to make a statement or form a conclusion.

## Key words

measurement
significance, calculation
result, conclusion, recommendation

## Example 1

In a tolerance question, you would need to calculate the upper and lower limits and use these to identify if, for example, parts were of an acceptable size.  ⇨

Cheryl buys bolts and nuts. The bolts have a diameter of 15 mm ± 2 mm. ————————

Alan sells Cheryl a drill bit with a diameter of 1·6 cm.

Explain why Cheryl may have a problem.

> When you see ± you should think of a tolerance type question, and begin to think of upper and lower limits and accuracy.

## Solution

The bolt diameter is 15 ± 2 mm.

lower limit = 15 − 2 = 13 mm

upper limit = 15 + 2 = 17 mm

The drill diameter is 1·6 ± 0·05 mm. ————

> No limit given, so take half of the smallest unit.

lower limit = 1·6 − 0·05 = 1·55 cm or 15·5 mm

upper limit = 1·6 + 0·05 = 1·65 cm or 16·5 mm

So a problem would occur when the bolt is at its upper limit (17 mm) because it would not fit in the drill hole, which has an upper limit of 16·5 mm.

## Example 2

Body mass index (BMI) is used to show if an adult is at a healthy weight.

The formula for calculating BMI is:

$$BMI = \frac{\text{weight in kg}}{(\text{height in metres})^2}$$

| BMI measurement | Category |
|---|---|
| Less than 18·5 | Underweight |
| Between 18·5 and 25 | Healthy weight |
| Between 25 and 30 | Overweight |
| Over 30 | Obese |

Dan is 1·87 m tall and weighs 93 kg.

In which category does Dan fall?

## Solution

$$BMI = \frac{\text{weight in kg}}{(\text{height in metres})^2}$$

$$= \frac{93}{1·87^2}$$

$$= 26·59$$

This means that Dan falls into the overweight category.

# Section 3.5 Justifying decisions based on measurements and calculations

## What you should know

★ You will be asked to use your working to justify a decision or recommendation.

## Key words

justify, conclude, recommend

## Example 1

A recipe for eight flapjacks needs 2 oz butter, 3 oz sugar and 4 oz rolled oats.

How many flapjacks can I make if I have 14 oz butter, 15 oz sugar and 16 oz rolled oats?

### Solution

There are different methods you could use.

For example:

● For a batch of eight flapjacks you need 2 oz butter. You have 14 oz, so you could make seven batches…but do you have enough of the other ingredients?

● For a batch of eight flapjacks you need 3 oz sugar. You have 15 oz, so you could make five batches.

● For a batch of eight flapjacks you need 4 oz oats. You have 16 oz so you could make four batches.

So the maximum number of batches you could make is four, giving $4 \times 8 = 32$ flapjacks.

## Example 2

Erin wants to replace her kitchen units.

She plans out her kitchen and the units would come to a total of £4000.

She is thinking of borrowing the money to pay for the units, and she has looked at three options:

● Option 1 — HP-R-Us Company offers hire purchase terms of a 15% deposit and 12 payments of £295.

● Option 2 — Avatar Loans offers no deposit and 24 payments of £180.

● Option 3 — Ipswich Loan Company offers no deposit and 36 payments of £117.

**a)** Which is the cheapest way to borrow the money?
**b)** Why may Erin decide to go with one of the other companies?

## Solution

**a)** HP-R-Us = 15% of £4000 + (12 × 295)

$$= 600 + 3540$$

total = £4140

Avatar = 24 × 180

$$= £4320$$

Ipswich = 36 × 117

$$= £4212$$

So HP-R-Us is the cheapest.

**b)** Erin may choose one of the others as the monthly payments are less (and therefore may fit better in a budget), and there is no deposit to pay. The overall cost is not hugely more expensive.

## Example 3

The manufacturer of a de-humidifier states that it reduces the moisture in the air by 70% every 3 hours.

A room was measured as having 4 litres of moisture in the air at 2 pm.

By 5 pm it was measured as having 1·3 litres of moisture.

Is the manufacturer's claim valid?

## Solution

There are various ways to answer this question.

For example:

70% of 4 l = 2·8

So the humidifier would have to remove 2·8 l (leaving 1·2 l).

However, there is 1·3 l left in the room.

So no, the manufacturer's claim is not valid.

*Or*

Find the percentage left in the room:

$$\left(\frac{1\cdot3}{4}\right) \times 100 = 32\cdot5$$

32·5% of the moisture is left in the room.

Which means 100 − 32·5 = 67·5% was removed.

This is less than the claim of 70%.

So no, the manufacturer's claim is not valid.

# Section 3.6 Extract and interpret data

## What you should know

★ At this level the information will be from at least three different graphical forms.

★ For example, there could be: a table, with at least five categories of information; a chart where the scale is not obvious; a graph where not all the data/values are given; a graph with part of an axis missing; a diagram such as a stem-and-leaf along with a scatter diagram or a map.

## Key words

table, graph, diagram, chart
category, data

## Example

Sara was comparing hire prices for a rotavator to dig up her garden. She obtained the following quotes from three companies:

- Basic Tool Hire — £80 per week or part of a week
- Green Gardeners — £50 for first day plus £10 each additional day
- Earth Works — £60 for first day plus £5 each additional day

Draw a graph to compare the costs from each company, and recommend which company Sara should place her order with if she thinks the job will take 4 days to complete.

### Solution

Draw a graph, with days along the horizontal axis and cost along the vertical axis.

- For Basic Tool Hire, plot (0, 80) and (7, 80). Join up with a (red) line.
- For Green Gardeners, plot (1, 50), (2, 60), (3, 70). Join up (green line) and extend.
- For Earth Works, plot (1, 60), (2, 65), (3, 70). Join up (blue line) and extend.   ⇒

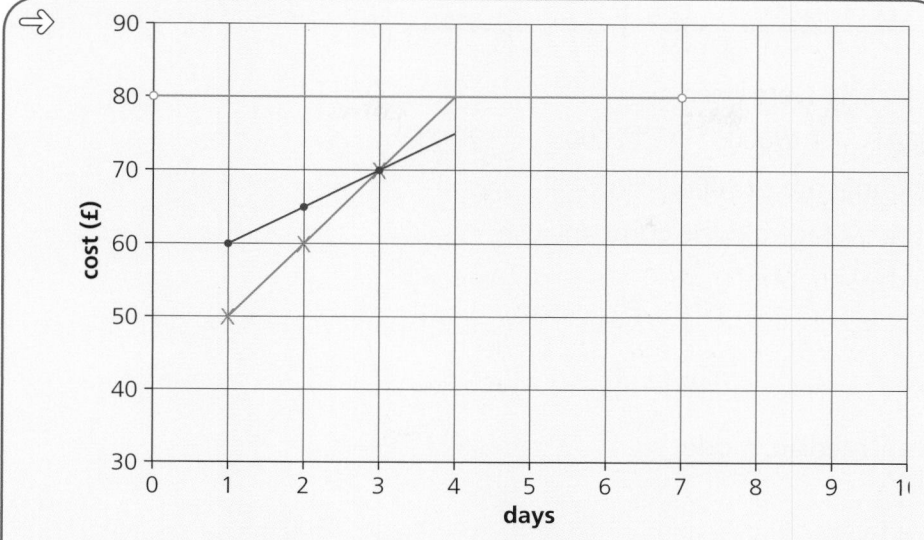

You can now advise Sara on which company to choose, depending on how many days she thinks she will require the rotavator for.

From the graph, it can be seen that Green Gardeners is cheapest for 1 or 2 days but Earth Works would be Sara's best choice for 4 days.

# Section 3.7 Make and justify decisions based on data

## What you should know

★ You will need to look for patterns or trends in data, use this evidence to justify a decision and to understand the effects of bias and sample size when making these decisions.

★ mean = $\dfrac{\text{total}}{\text{number}}$

★ mode = most common

★ median = middle (in order)

## Key words

pattern, relationship, trend
sample
bias

## Example

The incomes of six people in a factory were listed as:

£14 000 £16 000 £50 000 £16 000 £22 000 £20 000

The company states 'average earnings are £23 000'.

Which method of calculating the average did the company use?

Do you think this fairly reflects the situation?

### Solution

Key word: *average*

State each of the 'averages': mean, median, mode:

$$\text{mean} = \frac{\text{total}}{\text{number}}$$

$$= \frac{138\,000}{6}$$

$$= £23\,000 \quad\text{————— This was the value given.}$$

mode = £16 000 (it appears twice in the list)

median: 14 000 16 000 16 000 20 000 22 000 50 000

halfway between 16 000 and 20 000 = 18 000

So:

- the mean gives £23 000
- the mode gives £16 000
- the median gives £18 000

The mean of £23 000 is high because it has been impacted on by the outlier of £50 000.

The median more fairly represents the 'average'.

# Section 3.8 Make and justify decisions based on probability

## What you should know

- ★ How to recognise patterns and trends and use these to state the probability of an event happening. You will use this to justify decisions.
- ★ How to calculate the probability of combined events, and to identify possible bias.
- ★ Probability could be described using fractions, ratios, percentages and decimals, and again you need to use these to justify a decision.

## Key words

pattern, trend
probability, likelihood, combined
bias

## Example

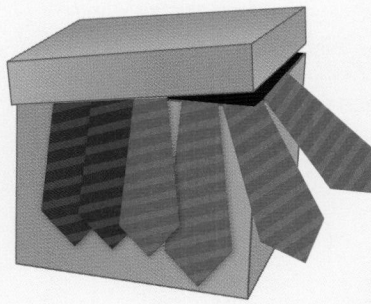

Neil and Wilma play a game. They put two blue ties and four red ties in a (closed) box. Neil wins if he pulls out two ties of the same colour. Wilma wins if she pulls out two ties of different colours.

Is the game fair?

## Solution

Perhaps a tree diagram would be good here, or calculating probabilities.

Neil would win if he picked B, B or R, R.

$P(\text{B, B}) = \dfrac{2}{6} \times \dfrac{1}{5}$ (six ties then five ties) $= \dfrac{1}{15}$

$P(\text{R, R}) = \dfrac{4}{6} \times \dfrac{3}{5} = \dfrac{6}{15}$

So Neil has a $\dfrac{7}{15}$ chance of winning (note this is less than ½, so already not fair).

Wilma would win if she picked B, R or R, B.

$P(\text{B, R}) = \dfrac{2}{6} \times \dfrac{4}{5} = \dfrac{4}{15}$

$P(\text{R, B}) = \dfrac{4}{6} \times \dfrac{2}{5} = \dfrac{4}{15}$

So Wilma has an $\dfrac{8}{15}$ chance of winning.

So the game is not fair because there is not an even chance of either winning.

### Hints & tips

$\dfrac{2}{6}$ because two of the six ties are blue, then $\dfrac{1}{5}$ because after one blue tie is removed there are only five ties, one of which is blue.

## Practice questions

1   Yasmin mixes up some lemonade in two glasses. In the first glass she mixes 200 ml of lemon juice and 300 ml of water.
In the second glass she mixes 100 ml of lemon juice and 200 ml of water.
Which glass is likely to taste more lemony?

2   The cost of a holiday at an outdoor centre depends on the time of year the holiday is taken and the number of nights staying at the centre. The table below shows these costs.

| Time of year | Cost |
|---|---|
| High season 1 May–30 Sep | £320 for 5 nights and £45 for each extra night |
| Mid season 16 Mar–30 Apr or 1 Oct–15 Nov | £270 for 5 nights and £40 for each extra night |
| Low season 16 Nov–15 Mar | £250 for 5 nights and £38 for each extra night |

Calculate the cost of staying at the centre for 9 nights beginning on 4 April.

3   Carr's soft drink company is changing the size of its bottles from 250 ml to 300 ml. Currently the 250 ml bottle of juice contains 25 g of sugar. How much will the new bottle contain?

4   Rachel knows she can complete her car journey in 3 hours when she travels at an average speed of 60 mph. Due to roadworks, her average speed is reduced to 50 mph. How long should Rachel allow for her journey?

5   Ian's scout group sells 1000 raffle tickets. Ian buys 15 tickets.
Ian's karate club sells 1200 raffle tickets. Ian buys 20 tickets.
In which raffle is Ian more likely to win a prize?

6   A medical practice surveyed 1500 children on its list to check on the measles, mumps and rubella (MMR) vaccination. The practice found a ratio of 4:1 for those who had received the vaccination.
How many children would the practice still need to vaccinate?

7   Trinity Academy offered a supported study class over an 8-week period. At the end of the 8-week period the school reviewed attendance to decide if the project was worth continuing. The results are shown below:

| Week | 1 | 2 | 3 | 4 | 5 | 6 | 7 | 8 |
|---|---|---|---|---|---|---|---|---|
| Attendance | 19 | 23 | 18 | 24 | 26 | 29 | 27 | 30 |

a) Draw a line graph to illustrate this information.
b) Describe the trend in attendance.
c) Would you recommend the school to continue with the project?

8   On a trip to Geneva, Carl books into a hotel, which costs him 600 Swiss francs. If the exchange rate is £1 = CHF1.25, how much did his hotel cost in pounds?

9  Carmen makes frames for pictures. She can make five frames in 1⅓ hours.
   How many frames could she make in 4 hours?

10 The table shows the ages and weights of 10 babies.

| Age (weeks) | 3 | 5 | 8 | 6 | 12 | 6 | 2 | 9 | 12 |
|---|---|---|---|---|---|---|---|---|---|
| Weight (kg) | 3·4 | 3·8 | 4·1 | 4·9 | 5·1 | 3·7 | 3·9 | 5 | 5·6 |

   a) Draw a scattergraph to show this information.
   b) Does there appear to be a correlation?
   c) If so, draw a line of best fit.
   d) Mary and John's baby is 7 weeks old. What would you expect the
      weight to be?

11 Kai has ⅔ of a litre of lemonade. He drinks ⅖ of it.
   What fraction of a litre did Kai drink?

12 James is a skipper of a fishing vessel.
   His quota of fish used to be 1200 tonnes.
   New regulations state that he must reduce his quota by 17%.
   What would be the limit of his quota now?

13 Andrew packed plates from a production line into boxes for distribution.
   If he broke more than 2% he would be given a reprimand.
   One week he packed 1440 plates and broke 26 of them. Would he have
   been reprimanded?

14 Calculate the area of the gable end of this house:

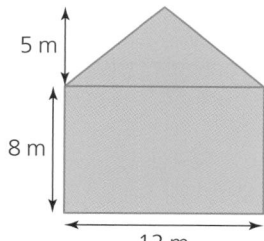

5 m
8 m
12 m

15 A cylindrical can of oil has to be able to contain ½ litre of oil.

   If the diameter of the can is 6 cm, what would be the minimum height of
   the can in order for it to hold the ½ litre of oil?

16 A trading standards officer recorded the amount of milk in 20 cartons
   taken at random from a milk depot. Her results are shown below.

   Contents of carton (ml):

   1001  1011  1005  1002  995  988  999  1000  1003  1007

   992  1010  989  1004  1000  1000  1005  997  1002  1003

   The cartons should contain 1 litre of milk.
   If 25% of the cartons are less than 1 litre, the depot would have to re-set
   the machines.
   Will the depot have to do this?

17 At the Beijing Olympics (2008), Germany and Slovakia won 12 medals
   between them in the canoeing events.
   ○ Germany won three gold and three bronze.
   ○ Slovakia won four medals in total — but none were bronze.
   ○ Between them, the two countries won three silver medals.
   a) Copy and complete this medal table:

|  | Gold | Silver | Bronze | Total |
|---|---|---|---|---|
| Germany |  |  |  |  |
| Slovakia |  |  |  |  |
| Total |  |  |  | 12 |

   b) If Germany chooses one of its Beijing 2008 medals at random, what is
      the probability that it will be a silver medal?

18 A 250 g packet of cereal contains 8 g of protein and 9 g of iron.
   What percentage of
   a) protein
   b) iron
   is in the packet of cereal?

19 The manufacturer of Derma Clean claims that, when sprayed onto a work
   surface, Derma Clean kills 75% of bacteria within 5 seconds.
   A work surface has 15 000 bacteria on it when Derma Clean is sprayed
   onto it.
   5 seconds later the bacteria number 3600.
   Is the manufacturer's claim valid?

# Chapter 4

# Examples of case studies

Paper 2 in the exam consists of case studies.

These are questions that follow a theme and will require you to combine skills and reasoning from across units, in a sustained way.

The paper will consist of a mixture of short, medium and long case studies.

Here are a few examples of case studies for you to practise.

## Practice case studies

1  Scotia Cars offers its sales people a choice of two methods of pay. Both methods have a basic pay plus a commission on their monthly sales.

| Scotia Cars | Deal 1 | Deal 2 |
|---|---|---|
| Monthly pay | £1250 | £950 |
| Rate of commission | 0·6% | 1·6% |

One month, Jennifer sold cars to the value of £40 250.
Which pay deal, 1 or 2, would pay her more for that month?        (5 marks)

2  While on holiday, James and his family want to hire a car. They see two adverts:
James has budgeted £250 for car hire.
With which company should he go to get most days for his money?
        (5 marks)

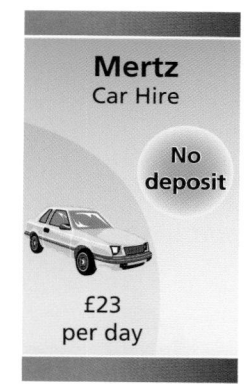

Mertz
Car Hire

No deposit

£23 per day

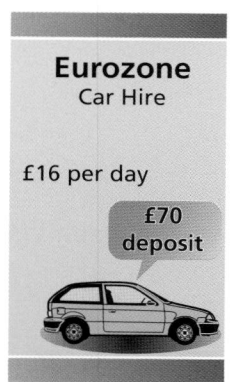

Eurozone
Car Hire

£16 per day

£70 deposit

3  The prices for an iPod in six different shops in Stirling are:
£66      £55      £70      £53      £61      £55
In six shops in Aberdeen the same iPod has a mean of £55 and a standard deviation of £2·60.
a)  For the shops in Stirling, calculate:
    i) the mean        (1 mark)
    ii) the standard deviation        (3 marks)
b)  Make two valid comparisons between the shops in Stirling and Aberdeen.        (2 marks)

4 A yacht leaves a harbour and sails for 40 km on a bearing of 040°.

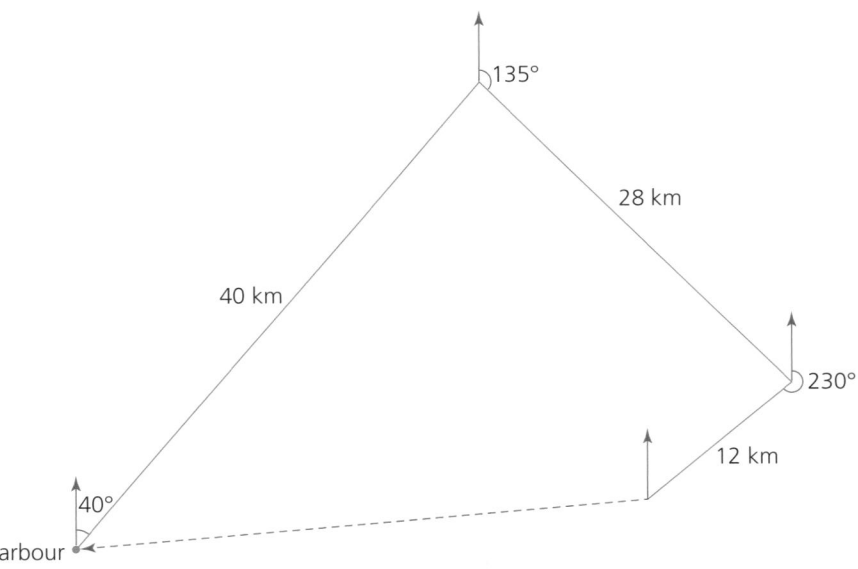

It then sails for a further 28 km on a bearing of 135°.
The third leg of the journey is 12 km on a bearing of 230°.
Construct a scale drawing, using a suitable scale, and use this to inform the captain of the yacht on what bearing, and for how far, he must sail to return to harbour. (8 marks)

5 Katy's Lunch Box Company makes lunch boxes in the shape of a cuboid with a lid formed from half a cylinder, as shown in the sketch.

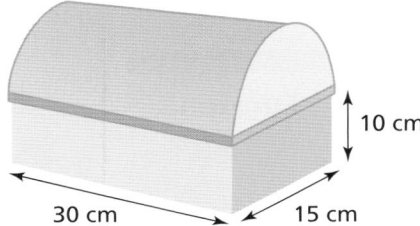

The boxes are packed into cardboard cartons for transport to the shops. The dimensions of the cartons are shown.

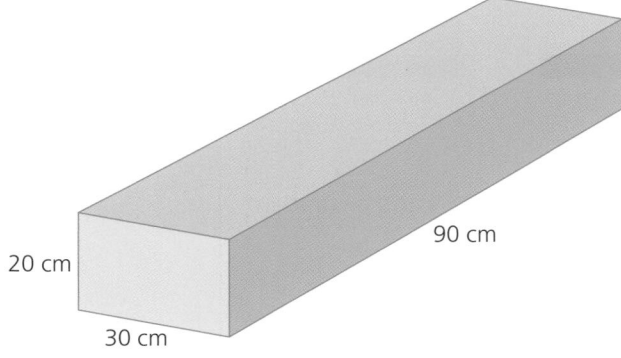

The cost of producing one lunch box is £2·15.
The transport cost per lunch box is £1·025.
The cost of one carton is £1·43.
The company receives an order from Noon's supermarket for 84 lunch boxes.

a) Calculate the volume of one lunchbox. (4 marks)
b) How many lunchboxes can be packed in the carton? (1 mark)
c) Calculate the total cost of producing the order of 84 lunch boxes, including the cartons required to transport them, and the cost of transporting the order. (4 marks)
d) Katy wants to make a 20% mark-up on the total cost. What will be the invoice to Noon's supermarket? (2 marks)
e) What should Noon's charge to ensure it makes a profit of at least 15% on each lunchbox? (3 marks)

6 When reading the weather and indicating temperatures, weather forecasters use a 'rough estimate' method of converting from Celsius to Fahrenheit. Mentally they *double the Celsius figure, then add 30° to get the Fahrenheit figure.* If the calculation was done accurately, the rule would be *multiply the Celsius figure by 9, then divide by 5, then add 32°.*
When reading the weather David says the temperature is 20°C.
a) If he estimated, what would he say the Fahrenheit temperature was? (1 mark)
b) How much out was he? (1 mark)
c) What is the minimum Celsius temperature for which the estimate would be the same as the accurate method? (3 marks)

7 Mr Smith is organising a sixth-year trip to Alton Towers.
There are 270 students in the sixth year.
He contacts Edinburgh Coach Services, which provides the following information regarding bus hire, cost and capacity.

| Type of coach | Capacity | Daily hire cost |
|---|---|---|
| Double-deck executive | 122 | £235 |
| Single-deck standard | 55 | £140 |
| Short-base coach | 18 | £75 |

Mr Smith is going to organise it so the largest coaches are filled first — and any spare seats will be in the final coach booked.

Using this system there are a number of possible options, some of which are shown in the table below. Three possible options have been completed.

| Double-deck executive | Single-deck standard | Short-base coach | Cost | Spare seats on final coach |
|---|---|---|---|---|
| 3 | 0 | 0 | £705 | 96 |
| 2 | 1 | 0 | £610 | 29 |
| 1 | 3 | | | |
| 1 | 2 | | | |
| 0 | | 0 | | |
| 0 | 4 | | | |
| 0 | 3 | 6 | £870 | 3 |

⇨
    a)  Complete the table to show all the different options.    (8 marks)
    b)  Which option is the cheapest?    (1 mark)
    c)  Which option wastes fewest seats?    (1 mark)
    d)  If Mr Smith chose the cheapest option, how much should he charge
        each student if he wanted to cover the costs plus about an extra 10%
        to allow for 'contingencies'?    (3 marks)

8  Rory is planning to paint the walls of his room with emulsion paint.
    The room is in the shape of a cuboid, with dimensions as shown.

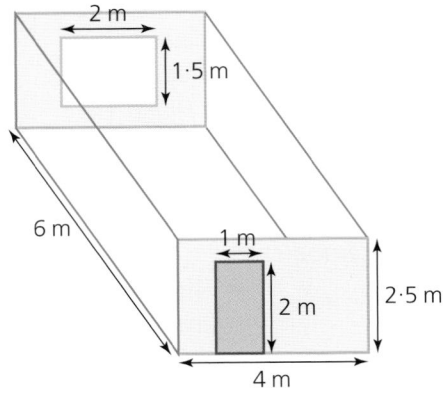

    Rory goes to a DIY store and sees this information about emulsion paint:

Emulsion
1 litre
Covers 16 m²

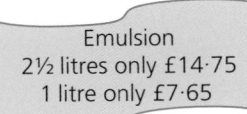

Emulsion
2½ litres only £14·75
1 litre only £7·65

    Given that the paint is only sold in 1-litre and 2½-litre tins, what is the
    minimum cost for Rory to paint his room?    (6 marks)

9  Planet Coffee blends its own coffee, and sells it in 1-kilogram packets.
    One blend consists of two kinds of coffee, Roma and Vivalto, which are
    mixed in the ratio 2:3.
    Roma costs £15 per kilogram and Vivalto costs £12.
    The shop has in stock 20 kg of Roma and 25 kg of Vivalto.
    a)  What is the maximum number of 1-kilogram packets of this blend
        that can be made?    (3 marks)
    b)  If the cost of the blend is in the same ratio as the mix, how much
        should the shop charge for 1 kilogram of blend, if it is to make a
        further mark-up of 5%?    (3 marks)

# Chapter 1 Managing finance and statistics

1 Basic pay = 40 × 8·20 = £328
  Overtime 5 hours @ 1½ = 5 × 12·30 = £61·50
  Overtime 4 hours @ 2 = 4 × 16·40 = £65·60
  His gross pay would be 328 + 61·50 + 65·60 = £455·10.

2 **a)** Text cost = £5
     Off peak calls = £1·50
     Peak calls = £3
     Total = £9·50, so balance of 50p remains
  **b)** New cost of texts is £6, so a deficit of 50p, or 50p over card balance

3 $\dfrac{£87·50}{50}$ = £1·75 per item

  Profit = £0·70 (2·45 − 1·75)

  Percentage is $\dfrac{0·70}{1·75} × 100 = 40\%$

4 1·2% × 700 = £8·40 for 1 year

  $\dfrac{7}{12} × 8·40 = £4·90$ for 7 months

5 **a)** Scattergraph drawn with biology on horizontal axis, chemistry on vertical axis
  **b)** Line of best fit drawn in
  **c)** Read from line of best fit (around 77%)

6 **a)** Allow 4° for each person $\dfrac{360}{90}$ :

|  |  |
|---|---|
| *Daily Bugle* | 45 × 4 = 180° |
| *Scotland Today* | 20 × 4 = 80° |
| Another | 15 × 4 = 60° |
| No paper | 10 × 4 = 40° |

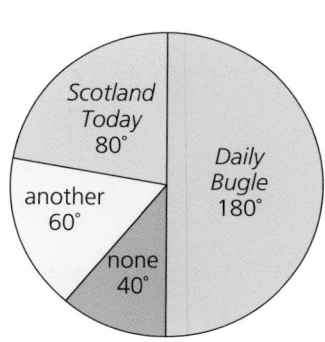

  **b)** $\dfrac{20}{90} = \dfrac{2}{9}$

7 15% of 2500 = £375

8 **a)** Construct a stem-and-leaf diagram:

| 0 | 6 | 7 | 8 |   |   |   |   |   |   |
|---|---|---|---|---|---|---|---|---|---|
| 1 | 0 | 2 | 3 | 4 | 7 | 7 | 7 | 8 | 9 |
| 2 | 1 | 3 | 4 | 4 | 5 | 7 |   |   |   |
| 3 | 1 | 1 | 2 | 6 | 6 | 9 |   |   |   |
| 4 | 1 | 5 | 5 | 6 | 9 |   |   |   |   |
| 5 | 0 |   |   |   |   |   |   |   |   |

**b)** Q1 = 17; Median Q2 = 24; Q3 = 36

**c)** Draw a box plot:

6    17    24    36    50

**9** $\dfrac{20}{100} = \dfrac{1}{5}$

**10 a)** mean = 71      sd = 1·69

**b)** Ted's scores are, on average, higher. However his scores are less consistent than Bill's.

**11** 13 000 × 0·88$^4$ = £7796

So, no, she should not expect to be able to sell the car for £9000.

**12** 120 000 × 1·08$^5$ = 176 319 bacteria = 180 000 to 2 sig. figs

**13** A pie chart would be a suitable diagram:

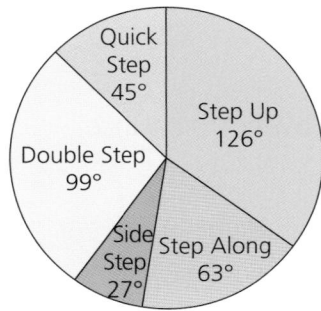

**14 a)** 35 37 42 42 42 80

mean = 46·3    median = 42    mode = 42

**b)** Choose either the mode or median as neither of these includes the outlier of 80.

# Chapter 2 Geometry and measures

**1  a)** 11·25 to 11·35

**b)** 90·5 to 91·5

Minimum of shelf is 90·5

Maximum of brick is 11·35

$\dfrac{90·5}{11·35} = 7·97 =$ not quite 8 bricks

**2** Cuboid: 16 × 16 × 25 = 6400

Cylinder: 3·14 × 64 × 25 = 5024

**3  a)** internal length = 2·29 m      internal width = 2·11 m

internal height = 2·06 m

**b)** 2·29 × 2·11 × 2·06

volume = 9·95 m$^3$

**c)** Base diagonal: $\sqrt{2·29^2 + 2·11^2} = \sqrt{9·7} = 3·1$ m  (Pythagoras)

Space diagonal: $\sqrt{3·1^2 + 2·06^2} = \sqrt{13·9} = 3·7$ m

4  a) Make a scale drawing
   b) Measure distance: 6·9 cm, so 6·9 km away
   c) Measure angle: 323°

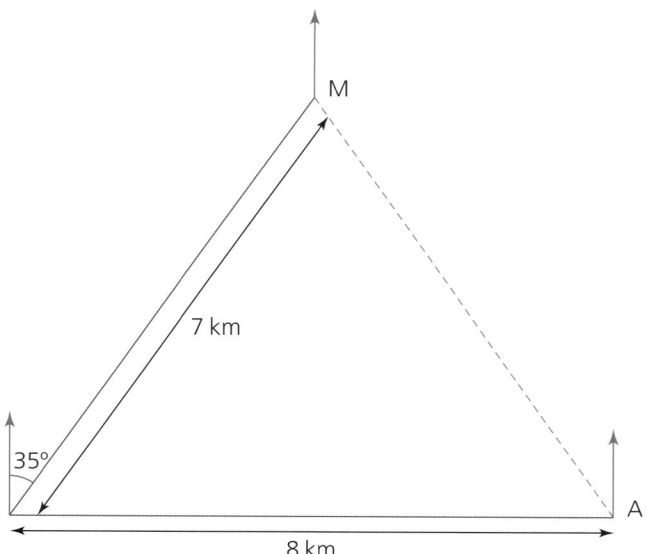

5  Ratio of 1 to 15, so 30 cm to (30 × 15) = 450
   Ramp to start 450 cm or 4·5 m away
6  Consider drawing a graph or trying values: −40° is the same in
   both °C and °F.
7  volume = cylinder + (2 × cones)
          = $\pi r^2 h + (2 \times \frac{1}{3}\pi r^2 h)$
          = 15·7 + 6·28
          = 21·98 cm³
8  a), b), c)

|  | Lower limit | Upper limit |
|---|---|---|
| Length | 21·95 | 22·05 |
| Width | 9·95 | 10·05 |
| Height | 7·95 | 8·05 |
| Area of face | 21·95 × 7·95 = 174·5025 | 22·05 × 8·05 = 177·5025 |
| Volume | 1736·3 | 1783·9 |

   d) When 'errors' are multiplied, the 'gap' is compounded.
9  area of face = 16 × 70 = 1120 cm²
   area of logo = 96 cm²

   percentage = $\frac{96}{1120} \times 100$

              = 8·6%
   This is acceptable as 8·6% < 10%.
10 area = $lb + \frac{1}{2}\pi r^2$
        = $(1\cdot4 \times 1\cdot2) + \frac{1}{2}\pi 0\cdot6^2$
        = 2·25 m²
11 Lower: 5·25 + 7·38 = 12·63
   Upper: 5·35 + 7·42 = 12·77

**12** Draw a scale diagram:

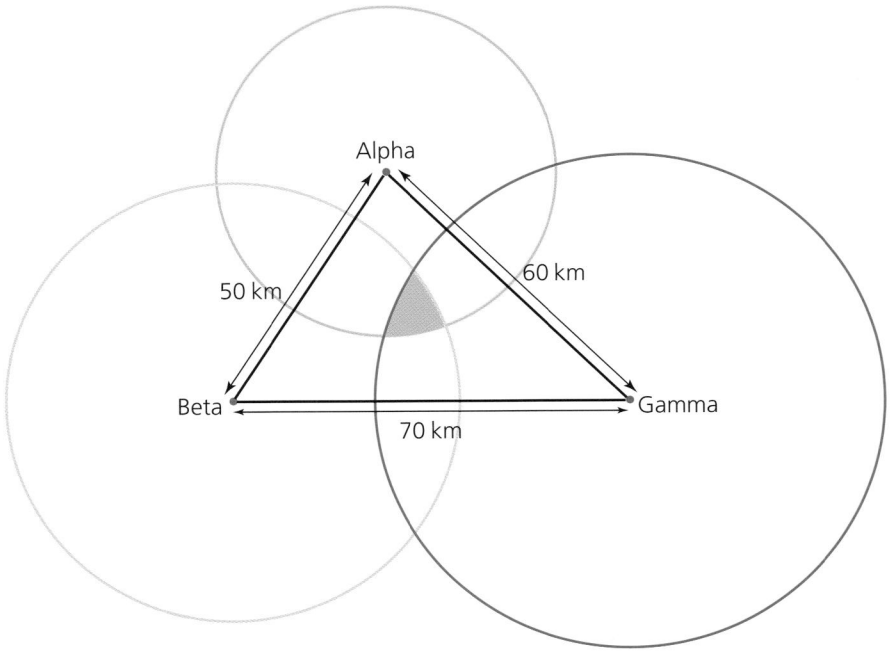

# Chapter 3 Numeracy and data

**1** First glass: 200 ml lemon to 300 ml water
Second glass: 100 ml lemon to 200 ml water
Difficult to compare, so make the amount of water equal.
Multiply 1st glass values by 2 and 2nd glass by 3 so that there will be 600 ml of water for comparison:
(200 ml/300 ml) × 2 gives 400 ml lemon to 600 ml water.
(100 ml/200 ml) × 3 gives 300 ml lemon to 600 ml water.
So the first glass will be more lemony because it has a greater proportion of lemon juice to 600 ml of water.

**2** 4 April is mid-season. Cost is 270 + (4 × 40) (270 for 5 nights then 4 more nights) = £430

**3** Direct proportion:

| Bottle size (ml) | Sugar (g) |
|---|---|
| 250 | 25 |
| 300 | More, so bigger number on top:<br>$25 \times \dfrac{300}{250} = 30$ |

30 g of sugar in new bottle

**4** Indirect proportion:

| Speed (mph) | Time (hours) |
|---|---|
| 60 | 3 |
| 50 | Longer, so bigger number on top:<br>$3 \times \dfrac{60}{50} = 3{\cdot}6$ hours |

Set aside 3 hours and 36 minutes for journey

5  $\dfrac{15}{1000} = 0.015$

$\dfrac{20}{1200} = \dfrac{1}{60}$ (0·0167), so this one has more chance of winning

6  Ratio of 4:1 $= \dfrac{1}{5}$ not vaccinated

$\dfrac{1}{5} \times 1500 = 300$

So 300 children still to be vaccinated.

7  a)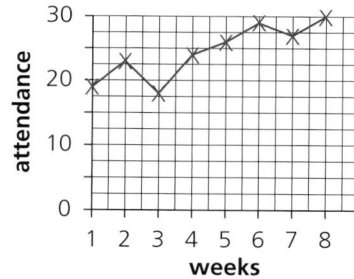

b)  The trend is upward — or the numbers are increasing.

c)  Yes, attendance is generally increasing so it is worth continuing.

8  $\dfrac{600}{1·25} = £480$

9  $1\dfrac{1}{3}$ hours for five frames

So in 4 hours: $\dfrac{(5 \times 4)}{\frac{4}{3}} = 5 \times 4 \times \dfrac{3}{4} = 15$

15 frames could be made.

10 a)  Draw a scattergraph.

b)  There does appear to be a correlation.

c)  Mark in a line of best fit.

d)  Read from your line.

11  $^2/_3 \times {}^2/_5 = \dfrac{4}{15}$ litre

12  $1200 \times 0.83 = 996$ tonnes

13  $\dfrac{26}{1440} \times 100 = 1·8\%$

So no reprimand, as 1·8 < 2

14  $8 \times 12 = 96\,\text{m}^2$ (rectangle)

$\dfrac{1}{2} \times 12 \times 5 = 30\,\text{m}^2$ (triangle)

So total area $= 126\,\text{m}^2$

15 Use the formula and work back:

$V = \pi r^2 h$

$500 = \pi \times 3^2 \times h$

$17·7 = h$

Height of container to be no less than 17·7 cm.

16 Six cartons contain less than 1 litre.

$\dfrac{6}{20} \times 100 = 30\%$

Machine to be reset, as 30% > 25%.

**17 a)**

| | Gold | Silver | Bronze | Total |
|---|---|---|---|---|
| Germany | 3 | 2 | 3 | 8 |
| Slovakia | 3 | 1 | 0 | 4 |
| Total | 6 | 3 | 3 | 12 |

**b)** $\dfrac{2}{8} = \dfrac{1}{4}$

**18** Protein $\dfrac{8}{250} \times 100 = 3.2\%$

Iron $\dfrac{9}{250} \times 100 = 3.6\%$

**19** $\dfrac{3600}{15\,000} \times 100 = 24\%$ left

Therefore 76% removed, so claim justified as 76% > 75%.

# Chapter 4 Examples of case studies

**1** Deal 1:
basic pay = £1250
commission = 0.6% × £40 250 = £241.50
total pay = £1491.50 ✓✓
Deal 2:
basic pay = £950
commission = 1.6% × £40 250 = £644
total pay = £1594 ✓✓
So for this month deal 2 would be the better deal. ✓

**2** Mertz car hire: number of days = $\dfrac{250}{23}$ = 10.87, so 10 days' hire is possible. ✓
Eurozone car hire: 250 − 70 = 180 ✓
$\dfrac{180}{16}$ = 11.25, so 11 days' hire is possible. ✓
(Correct round down) ✓
So James would be better to choose Eurozone if he wanted the greater number of days' hire. ✓

**3** Stirling shops:
mean = £60 ✓
standard deviation = £6.87 ✓✓✓
Aberdeen has a lower mean cost for the iPod, and the lower sd shows that the prices are more consistent across the Aberdeen shops. ✓✓

**4** For this case study you would get:
✓ for choosing a suitable scale — for example, 1 cm to 4 km
✓ for the first bearing and scaled line (accurate to ±2° and ±2 mm)
✓ for the second line and bearing (as above)
✓ for the third line and bearing
✓ for the return bearing and distance (including scaling up)

5  a) volume = cuboid + half cylinder ✓

$\qquad = lbh + \frac{1}{2}\pi r^2 h$ ✓

$\qquad = 4500 + 2649{\cdot}4$ ✓

$\qquad = 7149{\cdot}4\,\text{cm}^3$ ✓

   b) 6 boxes per carton ✓

   c) Cost = $(84 \times £2{\cdot}15) + (84 \times £1{\cdot}025) + (14 \times £1{\cdot}43)$ ✓ for 14 cartons (calculation) ✓✓

$\qquad = £286{\cdot}72$ ✓ total

   d) Mark up is $1{\cdot}2 \times £286{\cdot}72 = £344{\cdot}06$ ✓ for 1·2 (calculation) ✓

   e) Add 15% to £344·06 = £395·66 (round to £396) ✓

$\qquad \dfrac{£396}{84} = £4{\cdot}714 = £4{\cdot}71$; would give almost 15% profit ✓✓

   Rounding to £4·72 would give at least 15% profit.

6  a) Estimate = $(20 \times 2) + 30 = 70°\text{F}$ ✓

   b) Accurate = $(20 \times \dfrac{9}{5}) + 32 = 68°\text{F}$

   David's estimate was 2° higher. ✓

   c) Consider 30°C Estimate = 90    Accurate = 86

$\qquad\qquad$ 20°C Estimate = 70    Accurate = 68

$\qquad\qquad$ 10°C Estimate = 50    Accurate = 50

   (For 9°C the answers are 48 and 48·2.)

   So 10°C is the minimum temperature.

   ✓ Strategy — try some (e.g. 30°C converted, 20°C converted)

   ✓ Evidence of converting 10°C by estimate and accurately

   ✓ Evidence of converting values either side of 10, including one below 10° (e.g. 9°)

7  a)

| Double-deck executive | Single-deck standard | Short-base coach | Cost | Spare seats on final coach |
|---|---|---|---|---|
| 3 | 0 | 0 | £705 | 96 |
| 2 | 1 | 0 | £610 | 29 |
| 1 | 3 | 0 | £655 | 17 |
| 1 | 2 | 3 | £740 | 16 |
| 0 | 5 | 0 | £700 | 5 |
| 0 | 4 | 3 | £785 | 4 |
| 0 | 3 | 6 | £870 | 3 |

   ✓ for number of coaches in each line

   ✓ for cost/spare seats in each line

   b) Cheapest is 2, 1, 0 ✓

   c) Least wasted seats is 0, 3, 6 — but this is the most expensive ✓

   d) Cheapest is £610; add 10% = £671 ✓

$\qquad \dfrac{£671}{270} = £2{\cdot}485$ ✓

$\qquad\qquad = £2{\cdot}49$ per student ✓

   Mr. Smith would probably charge £2.50 to avoid giving 1 p change.

8  For calculating area of walls $(2 \times 4 \times 2.5) + (2 \times 6 \times 2.5) = 50$ ✓
   For calculating and subtracting window/door $(5) = 45\,\text{m}^2$ ✓
   For calculating litres required $(\div 16) = 2.8125$ ✓
   For rounding up $= 3$ litres ✓
   For knowing to choose $(1 \times 2\frac{1}{2}\,\text{l}) + (1 \times 1\,\text{l})$ (cheaper than 3 l) ✓
   For calculating cost: $(1 \times 2\frac{1}{2}\,\text{l}\ @£14.75) + (1 \times 1\,\text{l}\ @\ £7.65) = £22.40$ ✓

9  a)  Ratio is 2:3, so each kilogram contains 400 g Roma and 600 g Vivalto
       20 kg of Roma means $20 \div 0.4 = 50$ packets
       25 kg of Vivalto means $25 \div 0.6 = 41$ packets (calculation) ✓✓
       So maximum number of 1-kilogram packets of this blend is
       41 (communication) ✓
   b)  Calculate costs $= 41 \times 0.4 \times £15$   (Roma)    (strategy) ✓
                       $= 41 \times 0.6 \times £12$   (Vivalto)   (process) ✓
                       $= £541.20$
            Add 5% $= £568.26$
        Divide by 41 $= £13.86$   (process/communicate) ✓
       The shop should charge £13.86 per 1-kilogram packet.

# Overview of Lifeskills Maths National 4

The course comprises three component units: Managing finance and statistics, Geometry and measures, and Numeracy and data.

A fourth unit, the Added Value Unit, is assessed by means of a test.

To gain the course award you must pass all four units.

The units are assessed internally on a pass/fail basis within centres. National 4 courses are not graded.

The following table gives an outline of the course content for National 4 Lifeskills Mathematics and allows you to see how this progresses to National 5. Compare this with the table given in the introduction to this book on page v.

National 4 Lifeskills Mathematics

| Managing finance and statistics | Geometry and measures | Numeracy and data |
| --- | --- | --- |
| Finance:<br>● Budgeting for personal use or planning an event<br>● Balancing straightforward income and outgoings<br>● Income and deductions<br>● Determining the best deal given two pieces of information<br>● Currency exchange (two currencies, either direction)<br>● Interest rates<br>● Savings and borrowings | Geometry:<br>● Perimeter of shapes including rectilinear, circular and composite shapes<br>● Area of triangle, kite, rhombus, parallelogram, circle and composite shapes<br>● Volume of prism (including cuboid and cylinder)<br>● Solving a problem involving Pythagoras' theorem<br>● Using a scale factor on the dimensions of a shape | Numeracy:<br>● Significant figures/ decimal places<br>● Fractions/decimals/ percentages<br>● Speed/distance/time<br>● Area, perimeter and volume<br>● Ratio<br>● Proportion (direct)<br>● Measurements: recording, interpreting and explaining decisions |
| Statistics:<br>● Investigate risk and probability in context of lifestyles<br>● Statistics in diagrams, frequency tables, scattergraphs<br>● Draw a line of best fit | Measures:<br>● Calculate a quantity based on related measurements<br>● Construct a scale drawing with a given scale<br>● Plan a navigation course<br>● Container packing using first-fit algorithm<br>● Investigate tolerance<br>● Basic time management | Data:<br>● Extract/interpret data from at least two different forms<br>● Make and explain decisions based on interpreting data<br>● Make and explain decisions based on probability |

# Unit detail for Lifeskills Maths National 4

## Managing finance and statistics

The learner will use **reasoning and financial skills** linked to straightforward real-life contexts.

| | |
|---|---|
| Determining a financial position, given budget information | ● Budgeting and planning for personal use<br>● Balancing straightforward incomings and outgoings from a range of sources |
| Investigating factors affecting income | ● Investigating and interpreting income and deductions for personal circumstances and career choices. These could include:<br>  ● I Basic pay, gross/net pay<br>  ● Overtime<br>  ● Bonus<br>  ● Commission<br>  ● Benefits and allowances<br>  ● National Insurance<br>  ● Income tax |
| Determining the best deal, given two pieces of information | ● Comparing at least three products, given two pieces of information on each |
| Converting between currencies | ● Comparing costs between two different currencies in either direction |
| Investigating the impact of interest rates for savings and borrowing in a basic situation | ● These include:<br>  ● Loans<br>  ● Savings rates<br>  ● Bank accounts<br>  ● Credit agreements |

The learner will use **reasoning and statistical skills** linked to straightforward real-life contexts.

| | |
|---|---|
| Using statistics to investigate risk | ● Investigating the meaning of lifestyle statistics |
| Using and presenting statistical information in diagrams | ● Using and presenting straightforward statistical diagrams (technology may be used). These should include:<br>  ● Bar graphs<br>  ● Line graphs<br>  ● Pie charts<br>  ● Frequency tables without class intervals |
| Using diagrams to illustrate data | ● Emphasis on comparison and interpretation of graphs to include:<br>  ● Bar graphs<br>  ● Line graphs<br>  ● Pie charts<br>  ● Stem-and-leaf diagrams |
| Comparing data sets using mean and range | ● Using ungrouped data |
| Constructing a frequency table | ● Without class intervals |

| Constructing a scattergraph | ● From given or gathered data |
|---|---|
| Drawing a best fitting straight line on a scattergraph | ● Drawing a best-fitting line by eye<br>● Estimating one variable given the other<br>● Scattergraph should show a high positive or negative correlation |

# Geometry and measures

The learner will use **reasoning and measurement skills** linked to real-life contexts.

| Solving a basic problem in time management | ● Using time intervals to make plans, including across midnight |
|---|---|
| Calculating a quantity based on a related measurement | ● Any required formula(e) or relationship will be given |
| Constructing a scale drawing with a given scale | ● Scales expressed as a ratio or scaled line |
| Planning a basic navigation course | ● Using measurement of angles and length to interpret and to plan a straightforward navigation course |
| Carrying out container packing, using a first-fit algorithm | ● Filling containers in the order of arrival |
| Investigating the need for tolerance in a measurement | ● Accuracy up to two decimal places |

The learner will use **reasoning and geometric skills** linked to straightforward real-life contexts.

| Determining the gradient of a slope | ● Using 'vertical height' and 'horizontal distance' |
|---|---|
| Investigating a situation involving perimeter | ● To include:<br>  ● Rectilinear<br>  ● Circular<br>  ● Composite shape |
| Investigating a situation involving area | ● To include:<br>  ● Triangles<br>  ● Kite, rhombus, parallelogram<br>  ● Circle<br>  ● Composite shape |
| Investigating a situation involving volume | ● To include:<br>  ● Prism<br>  ● Cuboid<br>  ● Cylinder |
| Solving a problem involving the use of Pythagoras' theorem | ● Problems including calculating the length of:<br>  ● The hypotenuse<br>  ● A shorter side |
| Using a scale factor on the dimensions of a shape | ● Problems involving increase/decrease in an amount or measurement according to a scale factor |

# Numeracy and data

The learner will use **numerical skills** to solve straightforward real-life problems involving money, time and measurement.

| | |
|---|---|
| Selecting and using appropriate numerical notation and units | • Numerical notation to include =, +, −, ×, /, ÷, <, >, (, ), %, colon and decimal point<br>• Units should include:<br>  • Money (pounds and pence)<br>  • Time (months, weeks, days, hours, minutes and seconds)<br>• Measurement of:<br>  • Length (mm, cm, m, km, mile)<br>  • Weight (g, kg)<br>  • Volume (ml, l)<br>  • Temperature (Celsius or Fahrenheit) |
| Selecting and carrying out calculations | • Adding/subtracting whole numbers (including negative numbers)<br>• Multiplying whole numbers of any size with up to four-digit whole numbers<br>• Dividing whole numbers of any size by a single-digit number or by 10, 100<br>• Rounding answers to:<br>  • Nearest significant figure<br>  • Two decimal places<br>• Finding simple percentages and fractions of shapes and quantities<br>• Calculating percentage increase or decrease<br>• Converting between fractions/decimals/percentages<br>• Calculating rate<br>• Calculating distance given speed and time<br>• Calculating time intervals using the 12-hour and 24-hour clock<br>• Calculating:<br>  • Volume (cube and cuboid)<br>  • Area (rectangle and square) and<br>  • Perimeter (shapes with straight lines)<br>• Calculating ratio and direct proportion |
| Recording measurements using a straightforward scale on an instrument | • Using measuring instruments with straightforward scales to measure length, weight, volume and temperature<br>• Reading scales to the nearest marked, unnumbered division with a functional degree of accuracy |
| Interpreting measurements and the results of calculations to make decisions | • Using appropriate checking methods<br>• Interpreting results of measurements involving time, length, weight, volume and temperature<br>• Recognising the interrelationship between units in the same family, e.g. mm/cm, cm/m, g/kg and ml/l<br>• Using vocabulary associated with measurement to make comparisons for length, weight, volume, and temperature |
| Explaining decisions based on the results of measurements or calculations | • Giving reasons based on the results of measurements or calculations |

The learner will interpret **graphical data and situations involving probability** to solve straightforward real-life problems involving money, time and measurement.

| | |
|---|---|
| Extracting and interpreting data from at least two different straightforward graphical forms | • Straightforward graphical forms should include:<br>  • A table with at least four categories of information<br>  • A chart where the values are given or where the scale is obvious (e.g. a pie chart)<br>  • A graph where the scale is obvious (e.g. pie chart, bar graph, scattergraph or line graph)<br>  • A diagram (e.g. stem-and-leaf, map or plan) |
| Making and explaining decisions based on the interpretation of data | • Making decisions based on observations of patterns and trends in data<br>• Making decisions based on calculations involving data<br>• Making decisions based on reading scales in straightforward graphical forms<br>• Offering reasons for the decisions made based on the interpretation of data |
| Making and explaining decisions based on probability | • Recognising patterns and trends and using these to state the probability of an event happening<br>• Making predictions and using these predictions to make decisions<br>• Using relative frequencies and contingency tables, and describing probability through the use of percentages, decimal fractions and fractions, to make and explain decisions |

# Progressing from National 4 to National 5

The following tables show the progression, outcome by outcome, from Lifeskills Maths National 4 to Lifeskills Maths National 5.

# Managing finance and statistics

| Lifeskills Maths N4 | Lifeskills Maths N5 | Additional items (to N4) |
|---|---|---|
| Determining a financial position, given budget information | Analysing a financial position using budget information | ● Analysis<br>● Impact of change of an item |
| Investigating factors affecting income | Analysing and interpreting factors affecting income | ● Analysis<br>● Pension contributions |
| Determining the best deal, given two pieces of information | Determining the best deal, given three pieces of information | ● Three products with at least three pieces of information on each |
| Converting between currencies | Converting between several currencies | ● Either direction<br>● Use of at least three currencies in a multi-stage task |
| Investigating the impact of interest rates for savings and borrowing in a basic situation | Investigating the impact of interest rates for savings and borrowing | ● Credit cards<br>● Store cards<br>● More complex situations |
| Using statistics to investigate risk | Using a combination of statistics to investigate risk and its impact on life | ● Development of links between simple probability and expected frequency |
| Using and presenting statistical information in diagrams | Using a combination of statistical information presented in different diagrams | ● More complex statistical diagrams |
| Using diagrams to illustrate data | Using statistics to analyse and compare data sets | ● Constructing, interpreting and comparing:<br>  ● Box plots<br>  ● Scattergraphs<br>  ● Pie charts |
| Comparing data sets using mean and range | Using statistics to analyse and compare data sets | ● Calculating mean, median, range, inter-quartile range and standard deviation |
| Constructing a frequency table | – | – |
| Constructing a scattergraph | – | – |
| Drawing a best fitting straight line on a scattergraph | Drawing a line of best fit from given data | ● Drawing/interpreting a line of best fit<br>● Estimating from a line of best fit<br>● Comparing lines of best fit |

# Geometry and measures

| Lifeskills Maths N4 | Lifeskills Maths N5 | Additional items (to N4) |
|---|---|---|
| Solving a basic problem in time management | Solving a problem involving time management | ● Solving a problem in time management with some complex features including working across time zones |
| Calculating a quantity based on a related measurement | Calculating a quantity based on a two related pieces of information | ● More complex situations <br> ● Two related pieces of information |
| Constructing a scale drawing with a given scale | Constructing a scale drawing, including choosing a scale | ● Choosing a suitable scale |
| Planning a basic navigation course | Planning a navigation course | ● More complex navigation problems including bearings and length <br> ● Could include speed, distance, time |
| Carrying out container packing, using a first-fit algorithm | Carrying out efficient container packing | ● Assigning items to uniform containers to minimise amount of containers used <br> ● Best fit |
| Investigating the need for tolerance in a measurement | Considering the effects of tolerance | ● Effects of tolerance on, for example, areas, compatibility |
| – | Using precedence tables to plan tasks | ● Using precedence tables |
| Determining the gradient of a slope | Investigating a situation involving gradient | ● Including coordinates |
| Investigating a situation involving perimeter | – | – |
| Investigating a situation involving area | Solving a problem involving composite shapes including part of a circle | ● Part of a circle |
| Investigating a situation involving volume | Solving a problem involving the volume of a composite solid | ● Including fractional parts of solids, e.g. a hemisphere |
| Solving a problem involving the use of Pythagoras' theorem | Using Pythagoras' theorem within a two-stage calculation | ● Applying Pythagoras to, e.g. 3D (space diagonal) <br> ● Two-step calculation or within a context such as circle geometry |
| Using a scale factor on the dimensions of a shape | – | – |

# Numeracy and data

| Lifeskills Maths N4 | Lifeskills Maths N5 | Additional items (to N4) |
|---|---|---|
| Selecting and using appropriate numerical notation and units | Selecting and using appropriate numerical notation and units | • Simple formulae |
| Selecting and carrying out calculations | Selecting and carrying out calculations | • Working to two decimal places<br>• ×, / 1000 (2 d.p.)<br>• Rounding to three decimal places<br>• Using mixed numbers<br>• Finding fractional parts in a mixed number<br>• Compound percentage increase/decrease<br>• One quantity as a percentage of another<br>• Speed, distance, time<br>• Calculating volume (cylinder, triangular prism)<br>• Area (triangle, composite shapes)<br>• Perimeter (circumference)<br>• Ratio including dimensions from scale drawings<br>• Direct and indirect proportion |
| Recording measurements using a straightforward scale on an instrument | Recording measurements using a scale on an instrument | • Minor unnumbered division<br>• List as for N4, but including angle |
| Interpreting measurements and the results of calculations to make decisions | Interpreting measurements and the results of calculations to make decisions | • Identifying relevant measurements and results of calculations to make a decision |
| Explaining decisions based on the results of measurements or calculations | Justifying decisions by using the results of measurements and calculations | • Justifying<br>• Analysing<br>• Recommending |
| Extracting and interpreting data from at least two different straightforward graphical forms | Extracting and interpreting data from at least three different graphical forms | • A table with at least five categories<br>• A chart where all the values are not given or the scale is not obvious<br>• A graph where part of axis missing or scale not obvious<br>• A diagram, e.g. stem-and-leaf, scattergraph or map |
| Making and explaining decisions based on the interpretation of data | Making and justifying decisions using evidence from the interpretation of data | • Justify<br>• Patterns, trends and relationships in data<br>• Effects of bias and sample size |
| Making and explaining decisions based on probability | Making and justifying decisions based on probability | • Justify<br>• Recognise patterns, trends and relationships and use these to state the probability of an event happening<br>• Use evidence from the interpretation of probability to justify decisions<br>• Analyse the probability of combined events, identifying the effects of bias and describing probability through the use of percentages, decimals and fractions and ratio to make and justify decisions |